Also by R. Robin Baker

HUMAN NAVIGATION
AND
THE SIXTH SENSE

R. Robin Baker

SIMON AND SCHUSTER

NEW YORK

Published by Simon and Schuster
A Division of Gulf & Western Corporation
Simon & Schuster Building
Rockefeller Center
1230 Avenue of the Americas
New York, New York 10020
Originally published in Great Britain in 1981
by Hodder and Stoughton Limited
SIMON AND SCHUSTER and colophon
are trademarks of Simon & Schuster
Manufactured in the United States of America

10   9   8   7   6   5   4   3   2   1

Library of Congress Cataloging in Publication Data

Baker, Robin, date.
    Human navigation and the sixth sense.

    Bibliography: p.
    Includes index.
    1. Orientation.   2. Animal navigation.   3. Magnetic
fields–Physiological effect.   4. Senses and sensation.
I. Title.
QP443.B3   1981   152.1'882   81-16637
ISBN 0-671-44390-9   AACR2

To the memory of

PROFESSOR W. T. KEETON

His death in August 1980, at such an early age, leaves a great void in the field of animal navigation. Without his revolutionary work showing a role for the magnetic sense in pigeon navigation, the stage would not have been set for the parallel discovery of a similar sense in Man.

And

to all the students who took part in the Manchester and Barnard Castle experiments

Preface and acknowledgements

Over a century ago, in 1873, the journal *Nature* invited contributions on the mysterious and instinctive sense of direction in Man and other animals. There were many notable contributors, among them Charles Darwin. The articles crystallised a belief that has persisted in many quarters until the present day: animal navigation makes use of some form of 'sixth sense'. Paradoxically, at the same time that zoologists were proving beyond doubt that birds, amphibians, fish and many other organisms do indeed possess this sixth sense, a magnetic sense of direction, reaction against the possibility that Man possesses a magnetic sense was gaining momentum. Students of human navigation, finding no evidence for such a sense in the feats of pathfinders such as the Polynesians, were becoming strongly opposed to any such suggestion. Encouraged by the total absence of positive evidence and irritated by the steady flow of charlatans and tricksters seeking financial gain from claiming to have such a sense, the attitude amongst serious academics hardened against claims that Man might have a magnetic sense.

There the matter rested until experiments began in 1976 at Manchester University which tried simply to repeat as nearly as possible for humans the experiments that had successfully demonstrated a magnetic sense in other animals. Immediately, positive results were obtained. Appropriately, the first two papers on this work were sent to *Nature*, more than 100 years after the journal's initial invitation. Both were rejected. The first paper was never sent elsewhere. The second was eventually published by the American journal, *Science* (Baker 1980).

I have no doubt that the initial response to the parts of this book that deal with the human magnetic sense will be one of opposition and disbelief. Such opposition will be healthy and productive if it encourages people to attempt, with open minds, to repeat the experiments that the book describes. They are simple and cheap enough to carry out, well within the resources even of most schools, as well as colleges and Universities. An appendix is added specifically to assist University lecturers and schoolteachers, with no previous experience in navigation work, to carry out and analyse such experiments using their own students. Only when many people have seen for themselves the influence of changed magnetic fields on the human sense of direction will the existence of a magnetic sense be accepted.

At first, the possibility that humans have a magnetic sense seems incredible. Throughout this book I have discussed the evidence for humans side by side with the evidence for other animals. I maintain that, when placed in this wider perspective, it would be incredible if Man did not have a magnetic sense. Even so, I have no doubt that the conclusion will still be resisted for one reason and one reason alone: the sense is an unconscious one and in the minds of many people, therefore, cannot exist. Indeed, one influential member (who shall be nameless) of the scientific community went so far as to tell me: 'We know humans do not have a magnetic sense otherwise we should feel it. So whatever your results show it isn't that.' In this book I suggest that humans are not alone in having a magnetic sense that is unconscious. Moreover, I suggest that the primary role of the sense in Man and other animals is dependent on that unconsciousness.

Initial reaction to this book will inevitably revolve around response to its claims regarding the magnetic sense. There is, however, a second theme, the implications of which should endure long after final acceptance of the human magnetic sense has become history. I know I am not alone in my irritation with the sociobiology debate that currently bedevils the study of behavioural ecology. It is my earnest wish that behaviourists be allowed to continue their studies away from the distractive and destructive battlefields of ideological warfare. Continuing philosophical and ideological debate over whether behaviourists are justified in studying Man and other animals side by side inevitably reduce solely to dogma and politics. As such, the debate is circular, counterproductive—and largely unnecessary. In this book, using navigation as my theme, I have attempted to show that if ideology and dogma are set aside and behaviourists simply get on with the task of studying Man and other animals each in the perspective of the other, practical and academic benefits come tumbling out.

I am extremely grateful to Edward Broadhead of Leeds University and Susan Devlin who, as biological editor and editor respectively for Hodder and Stoughton, have given me the opportunity to present data and views that will inevitably cause a strong and, I suspect, not always favourable reaction. I am particularly grateful to Hodder and Stoughton also for offering to publish the book quickly so that it appears not too long after the first news of the discovery of the magnetic sense in humans has broken in the scientific and popular press.

My major thanks must, of course, go to all the students involved in the navigation experiments, to whom this book is partly dedicated: Yorkshire Television suggested and financed the Barnard Castle experiments and David Bellamy in his own inimitable way added bizarre touches to a unique experiment. Stuart (Bill) Bailey designed the helmets used in the Manchester experiments and he, Janice Mather, and Nigel Stone helped take the compass bearings and other data during the Series III experiments. I am further grateful to Jan for all the discussions and encouragement in the pursuit of this work and particularly for her confident assertion that the Barnard Castle magnet experiment would produce positive results at a time when I was strongly tempted to postpone such a pioneer experiment until a less public occasion. I was assisted during the Barnard Castle experiments by staff from the schools that provided the sixth-form students. Tricia Munn drew my attention to the Juanita Núñez episode in *The Moneychangers*.

This book was written in the space of four weeks in February and March 1980, working for seven days a week, often for 18 hours a day. Such intensive activity would not have been possible without the continuing uncomplaining forbearance of my wife and children. My final acknowledgement, however, is to the composer, Mozart, and the band, Blondie. Their music, in just about equal proportions, served two functions without which the book could not have been written in the time available. First, it drowned the distractive ambient sounds that invade (and emanate from) our house in Bramhall. Secondly, it replaced them with an aesthetic and stimulating atmosphere that, more so even than endless coffee, allowed such intensive and lengthy writing, analysis and illustration.

Manchester   Robin Baker

Contents

Human Navigation
and the Sixth Sense

1

Introduction

On 29 June 1979 at Barnard Castle, England, a group of 31 sixth-form pupils climbed on board a coach in their school car park and blindfolded themselves. They placed magnets on their heads, settled back in their seats, and started to concentrate. Through steady drizzle, the coach travelled tortuously through the town centre before emerging onto a fairly straight trunk road and setting off for the southwest. After 5 km or so, the vehicle stopped briefly, then turned through 135° and set off eastwards to a second position, this time 5 km southeast of the school. At each stop the passengers were asked, while still blindfold, to write on a card an estimate of their current compass direction from school. After the second stop, the cards and magnets were collected and later examined. The pattern that emerged was as dramatic as it was unexpected.

All the passengers had thought they were wearing magnets. In reality, half of them had been wearing brass bars, magnetically inert but otherwise similar in size, shape and colour to the real magnets. Analysis showed that whereas the group wearing brass bars could produce a statistically acceptable written estimate of 'home' direction from both sites, the group wearing magnets could not. The results implied that the ability to judge direction when blindfold was disrupted by placing a magnet on the head. This in turn implied that people have a magnetic sense of direction; a 'sixth sense'.

The Barnard Castle experiment was the first serious work to provide positive support for the existence of a magnetic sense of direction in humans. In so doing, it supported a suggestion that, in fact, is not as ancient as many people might suppose. The term 'sixth sense' itself was not coined until 1905 and the suggestion that Man might possess an unconscious sense of direction probably goes back no further than the early–to mid-nineteenth century (Gatty 1958).

Until 1976, the study of human navigation had been the domain of psychologists, anthropologists, geographers and architects. In that year the first experiments were carried out using the techniques developed originally to study navigation in other animals, notably Homing Pigeons, **Columba livia**. The Barnard Castle experiment itself was a direct attempt to replicate for humans experiments that had successfully demonstrated a magnetic sense of direction in pigeons.

These first experiments on human navigation showed in a dramatic way the benefits that could be gained from the application of zoological techniques to the study of human behaviour. At the same time, the results obtained for humans suggested new perspectives for an understanding of animal navigation in general. Suddenly, the intriguing possibility presented itself that a detailed study of humans could well give valuable insight into the navigational abilities of other animals; abilities that for so long have been incredibly resistant to experimental evaluation.

These then are the two major themes of this book: (1) the application of zoological techniques to the study of Man; and (2) the mutual benefits that arise when the navigational mechanisms of humans and other animals are studied, each in the perspective of the other. Not least among these benefits, the vast experience that has accrued from the design of navigation experiments on other animals is invaluable in the design of experiments suitable for the study of humans (Chapter 3). Identification of the principal mechanisms in navigation (Chapter 4), however, owes as much to an appreciation of human techniques as of those shown by other animals. In general, navigation involves two separate, but complementary, mechanisms and these allow the results of

Fig. 1.1 Moroccan caravan crossing desert

How do humans explore and pioneer new routes from one place to another without losing their way? Thereafter, what environmental clues do they use to travel this new route time and time again in different seasons and in different weather conditions? Are humans more or less accomplished at such navigation than other animals, such as, say, camels? These and similar questions are at the heart of the study of human navigation.

(Photo Courtesy of John Topham)

navigation experiments to be considered in two parts. First, there is analysis of the new-found ability of Man and other animals to estimate the outward journey, even when unable to see (Chapter 5), and the dramatic evidence for the involvement of a magnetic sense of direction in this ability (Chapter 6). Secondly, there is the question of how much this first estimate improves or deteriorates once the subject is allowed to see the surroundings at its destination and the extent to which this reassessment is influenced by weather, visibility, topography, and so on (Chapter 7). Once these major elements in navigation have been determined experimentally for humans, they can be incorporated into the less rigorous anthropological data (Chapter 8). At the same time, the navigational mechanisms employed by people such as the Amerindians, Australian Aborigines, and Polynesians can be compared with the navigational mechanisms employed by other animals.

Previously, students of human navigation have found it unnecessary to postulate the existence of a magnetic sense in order to explain the pathfinding abilities of the natural navigators of the world (Fig. 1.1). This fact does little to aid the credibility of the magnetic sense. Chapter 9 discusses the role of the magnetic sense in natural navigation and suggests why this sense and its role may be unconscious.

When considering the long-distance navigation of humans, it soon becomes apparent that such behaviour is primarily a male domain. Perhaps the most contentious issue in the entire study of human navigation, apart from the existence of a magnetic sense, is the possibility of differences in the abilities of males and females (Chapter 10), the subject for discussion during many a family outing. The book ends (Chapters 11 and 12) by considering the relevance of navigation experiments to natural navigation and by discussing the evolutionary implications of the similarity between the navigational systems of Man and other animals. It begins, however, by considering just what we mean by navigation (Chapter 2).

2

What is navigation?

The word 'navigation' means different things to different people. For most it refers to the methods of determining the position and course of a ship or aircraft by some combination of geometry and astronomy. The navigation system of most modern jets, however, is based on inertial navigation; a gyroscopic, dead-reckoning system that calculates position by summing all the twists and turns of the journey. Astronomy is not involved. In everyday use, the passenger in a car may be asked to navigate by following a map and looking for road signs while the person behind the wheel concentrates on driving. Most zoologists automatically associate navigation with the long-distance migrations of animals such as birds and fish and their spectacular ability to return to a particular nesting or spawning site after a round trip of perhaps several thousand kilometres. Alternatively, the word may be associated with Homing Pigeons and their equally spectacular ability to return home when taken to some unknown site and released perhaps hundreds of kilometres away.

Varied though these uses of the word 'navigation' may appear at first sight, they do seem to have two elements in common: (1) familiarity with the destination or goal; and (2) a lack of familiarity with the route or terrain between this goal and the present position. These two elements together separate navigation from otherwise similar mechanisms. Mariners, for example, distinguish between a navigator and a pilot. A navigator finds his way to a goal across waters that are unfamiliar. A pilot, on the other hand, is a person taken on board specifically because he has an intimate local knowledge and is familiar with the waters to be negotiated. Taking our cue from this distinction, **navigation** is the method of determining the direction of a familiar goal across *unfamiliar* terrain whereas **pilotage** is the method of determining the direction of a familiar goal across *familiar* terrain.

Both pilotage and navigation are forms of **goal orientation**. They are to be contrasted with **orientation** (Fig. 2.1) which is concerned solely with direction and not with destination. When an animal is seen travelling in a purposeful manner across country in a straight line, there is only one way to determine whether it is showing orientation or goal orientation and that is by displacing it sideways. If, after displacement, the animal continues parallel to its original track, then it is showing orientation. If, on the other hand, it appears to compensate for the displacement and continues to travel toward a particular destination, then it is likely to be showing goal orientation (Fig. 2.1). As their names suggest, however, the distinction between orientation and goal

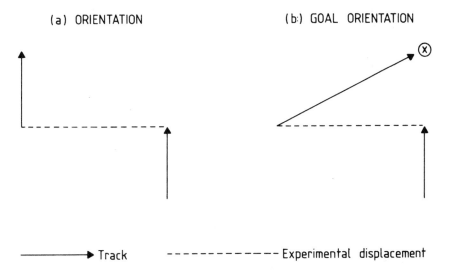

(a) ORIENTATION   (b) GOAL ORIENTATION

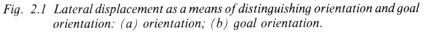

————————▶ Track   ———————————— Experimental displacement

Fig. 2.1 Lateral displacement as a means of distinguishing orientation and goal orientation: (a) orientation; (b) goal orientation.
(Modified from Baker 1978)

orientation may not always be quite as clear-cut as Fig. 2.1 might imply. Consider the displaced individual in Fig. 2.1 b. Goal orientation can be very brief. Once the individual has decided that its goal is northeast of its present position, it can reach that goal solely by orientation. In order to study the goal-orientation mechanism, therefore, whether navigation or pilotage, it is necessary to study the animal at the time it is making its decision about home direction. To study it after that time is to risk studying only orientation, not goal orientation. As the mechanisms involved in maintaining a particular direction are quite different, and usually much simpler, than those involved in calculating the direction of a goal, then it is important to design experiments so that the two mechanisms are studied separately.

Given these definitions of goal orientation, navigation and pilotage, it follows that animals need to navigate whenever they find themselves separated from their familiar goal by a stretch of unfamiliar terrain. Under what circumstances is an animal likely to find itself in such a situation? The answer lies with exploration and the process of familiarisation.

All vertebrates, when adult, seem to organise their lives around familiarity with their environment (Baker 1978, 1981a). Each individual has its own **familiar area** within which it knows where and when it is best to go in order to obtain or do this or that. Like humans, however, the adults of other vertebrates are familiar with more places than they actually use during the course of a day, month or even year. Indeed, some familiar sites will never again be visited.

The part of an individual's familiar area that it actually uses is known as its **home range**. By and large, the reason the home range of a human is smaller than his or her familiar area is because many familiar places are no longer as productive or as convenient as others and so are no longer worth visiting. In effect, therefore, as the human assesses which places are good and which are bad, adopting the former but rejecting the latter, a relatively small home range crystallises out from the larger familiar area. This same process of building up a large familiar area followed by crystallisation of a smaller home range as a result of habitat assessment seems to be common to all vertebrates (Fig. 2.2).

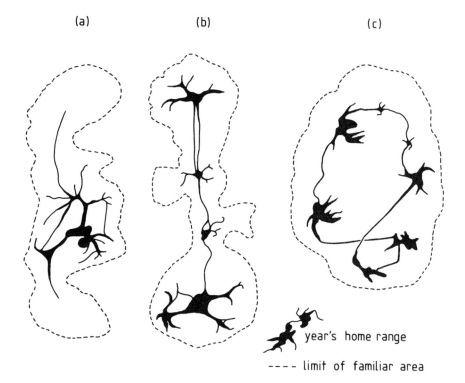

Fig. 2.2 Three types of year's home range: (a) static home range; (b) seasonal to-and-fro return migration; (c) annual migration circuit

Solid black shows the area used by an animal during the course of a year. The dashed line marks the limits of the familiar area built up by the animal when younger. In effect, no matter what the form of the year's home range, it crystallises out from a much larger familiar area.

When an individual, human or otherwise, is born, it has no familiar area. By the time it is adult, its familiar area is large. How is familiarisation achieved? Some information may be collected by social communication, particularly in humans, either by word of mouth or from magazines, books, etc. None of these methods, however, is a suitable substitute for direct experience; for **exploration**. At intervals the individual travels, either solitarily or in the company of others, through unfamiliar areas and incorporates the new places visited within its expanded familiar area.

Figure 2.3 illustrates a typical exploratory foray beyond the current limits of an individual's familiar area. In order to explore efficiently, the individual has to overcome two major difficulties. First, it has to avoid becoming lost. Secondly, it has to incorporate any new and suitable site that it encounters into its home range. The simplest way to meet both of these difficulties would be, of course, to retrace the outward journey and to use the same route on all future visits. Unless this journey was straight, however, such route-reversal is unlikely to produce an efficient track. Clearly, there is an advantage in being able to pioneer the most economical route back to some point within the current home range (dotted line in Fig. 2.3). How can the direction of this route be determined from the new site? The answer, of course, is by navigation.

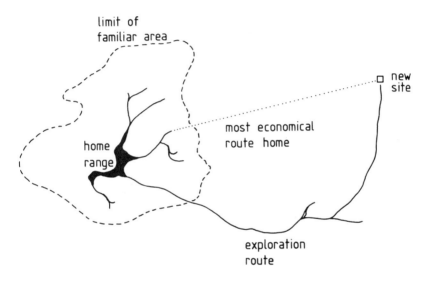

Fig. 2.3 When an animal explores, the direction of the most economical route home can be determined only by navigation.

Any species that shows exploration, therefore, should have been acted upon by natural selection for the existence and refinement of an ability to navigate. Since all vertebrates explore, it follows that we should expect all vertebrates, including Man, to have some level of navigational ability. Humans build up a familiar area by exploration and there can be no doubt that throughout most of Man's evolution the costs of becoming lost when exploring or of taking unnecessarily long and difficult routes between sites have been as great as for any other animal. Consequently, natural selection for an ability to navigate has been equally intense. There may, however, have been a difference in intensity on males and females.

Man shares with other primates and some other social species, such as various ungulates, an apparent sexual difference in the expression of exploratory behaviour (Baker 1978). In all human cultures, males are more likely to set off on long, solitary explorations than females. Given such a difference there may well have been differential selection on navigational ability in the two sexes.

Modern Man still needs to be able to navigate. Whenever a person finds himself or herself in unfamiliar surroundings, a navigation mechanism is implemented. In many parts of the world, however, such as western Europe, there are so many aids to navigation (e.g. maps, compasses, road signs, place names, other people) that even if the resident humans did have an innate ability to navigate without instruments, they would rarely need to use it. Such navigational aids, however, have only been available to large numbers of people for a relatively short time, even in western Europe; perhaps three or four generations at the most. Throughout most of human evolution, navigation without instruments has been the rule. Furthermore, use of such an ability must have been frequent, particularly by males and particularly during adolescent exploration (Baker 1978, 1981a,b), and the consequences of poor navigation must surely have been dire. Even for modern industrialists we may wonder whether an individual is perhaps more vulnerable when in an unfamiliar area.

This combination of a long evolutionary history of selection for an ability to navigate yet the modern lack of opportunity or necessity to develop and use the ability is experimentally both an advantage and a disadvantage. On the one hand, any positive results for navigational proficiency with naïve subjects could well largely reflect an innate ability. On the other hand, not only is the existence of the ability more difficult to demonstrate but also its potential accuracy cannot be studied without putting the subjects through an intensive training programme. Even this may be no substitute for everyday use of the ability during early life.

The first step, however, is to design an experiment that allows us to evaluate whether Man does have the ability to navigate without using instruments. Only then can the mechanisms involved in such an ability be investigated and the response to training programmes evaluated. This design is the concern of the next chapter.

3

How to demonstrate
navigation

Until recently, experiments on the spatial sense of humans have been carried out by psychologists and there is a large literature (see Howard and Templeton 1966, Canter 1977). Typically, most such experiments have been in relatively confined spaces, usually indoors, and have required the subjects to judge angles and distances relative to artificial targets. Such experiments tell us a great deal about the human senses and are beginning to give some insight into the way Man stores spatial information within the central nervous system (O'Keefe and Nadel 1979). It is dangerous, however, to extrapolate from this type of experiment to the navigational techniques used by humans when exploring beyond the limits of their familiar area. Senses and mechanisms appropriate to the calculation of the direction of distant goals in the outside world may be quite different from those employed in making fine angle and distance judgements in confined spaces. For example, in a series of experiments on Homing Pigeons, Whiten (1978) showed that, when a bird is restrained in a box and given a stable horizon, it is able to use the sun's altitude to make judgements about the direction of its home loft. The available evidence, however, suggests that the sun's altitude is not part of the navigational mechanism employed by birds allowed to fly freely (Schmidt-Koenig 1979). We can only fully be satisfied with experiments on humans, therefore, if they involve displacements over distances that would normally be covered during exploration. In other words, we need to adopt the methods that zoologists have employed for decades in the study of the navigation of other animals. Having done so, we can then compare the results with those obtained by psychologists. We should hope that there will be many similarities but it is a fairly safe prediction that there will also be many differences. The first step in designing navigation experiments on humans, therefore, is to make use of the experience gained over the years in experiments on other animals.

Traditionally, zoologists have experimented on navigation by displacing animals to some unfamiliar site, releasing them, and observing their response. This method closely mimics the process of exploration (Fig. 3.1) and it is reasonable to suppose that it requires the animals to employ the same navigational mechanisms as during natural exploration over a comparable distance through the same terrain. In both they should try to pioneer the most economical route back to their usual home range.

There was a time, in the first half of the twentieth century, when almost all navigation experiments were **homing experiments**. Indeed, studies on some

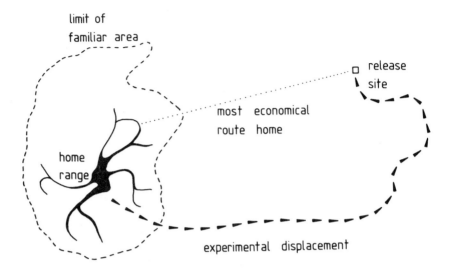

Fig. 3.1 Displacement/release experiments mimic natural exploration

groups of animals, such as bats and other terrestrial mammals, are only just moving out of this phase, and most people not actively involved in the study of navigation probably imagine that homing is still the primary experimental technique. In homing experiments, a group of animals are displaced to some unfamiliar site, released, and the proportion that returns home and the rate at which they do so is monitored. Either or both of these measures represent **homing success**. However, navigation is no longer studied in this way.

There are several reasons for abandoning homing success as the measure of navigational ability, though most reduce to the fact that it is rarely a measure solely of navigation. As an extreme example, consider an experiment in which a group of snails is displaced to a point 100 km from their home range. We may safely predict that their homing success will be zero. This tells us little, however, about their ability to determine the direction of home from such a distance, only that they are unable to travel long distances. A less extreme example of a similar principle is a well-known feature of navigation experiments on small mammals. When rodents are displaced from their home range and released, a proportion, often as high as 30 per cent, apparently makes no attempt to return. Instead they establish themselves near to the point of release (Bovet 1978). Moreover, the proportion that fails to home increases with distance of release. It could be argued that such behaviour reflects a decreasing ability to work out the home direction as distance from home increases. On the other hand, it could be argued that the rodents always know where they are on release and that it is precisely because they do know where they are, a long way from home, that they make no attempt at the return journey.

A decreased motivation to return with increased distance of release could be one factor in what has been shown many times for many different animals to be the chief characteristic of homing experiments: that homing success

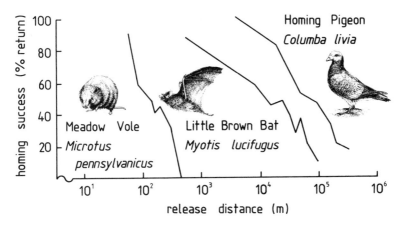

Fig. 3.2 Homing success declines with increase in release distance (Simplified from Bovet 1978)

decreases with increasing distance between the release site and home (Fig. 3.2). Another factor that would produce the same effect, and again one that has little to do with navigational ability, is that of predation risk. The further an individual has to travel before it arrives back at its familiar area, the more likely it is to suffer accident or predation. The most important factor in the eventual abandonment of homing success as a measure of navigational ability, however, was the realisation that a decline with distance could indicate that animals have no navigational ability at all but home instead by random search.

If a group of animals were to be released at a site from which none of them could determine the direction of home, we might nevertheless expect a lucky few to return simply because they happened by chance to set off in the correct direction. Mathematical models have been produced to show that random search could account very well for the observed homing success of birds (Wilkinson 1952) and salmon (Saila and Shappy 1963) and for a time there seemed a real possibility that animals had no navigational ability and that all homing occurred by chance.

It was not difficult, however, to design experiments to prove that an ability to navigate existed and that homing was not simply the result of random search. The technique, instead of measuring homing success, was to observe animals immediately after release. Two major methods were developed. The first, used for conspicuous animals such as Homing Pigeons, involved recording the direction of the **vanishing point**, the last observed position of an animal after release (Matthews 1955). The second method, developed for animals such as smaller birds (e.g. Bank Swallows/Sand Martins, **Riparia riparia** (Sargent 1962)), amphibians (Ferguson 1971), and small mammals (Mather and Baker 1980), that after release could not easily be watched, was to restrain the animals at the release point in some form of **orientation cage**. Such cages (e.g. Fig. 3.3) were designed to allow the experimenter to record the directional preferences of the animal. Such preferences are manifest either as

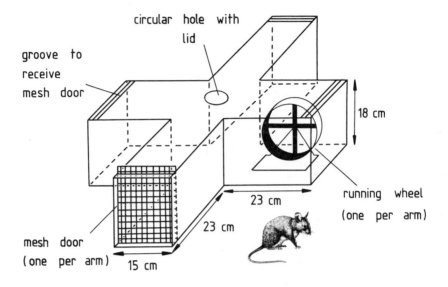

Fig. 3.3 Perspex orientation cage used to study navigation by small rodents
At the release point, an animal was introduced into the apparatus through the
circular hole. The time spent in each arm was recorded and analysed for
directional preference.
(Simplified from Mather and Baker 1980)

more-frequent movements in some directions than others or as more time spent in some directions than others. In effect, through the design of the orientation cage, the experimenter is encouraging the animal to 'point' the direction in which it would depart if it were to be released. Such techniques allow an animal to betray that it 'knows' the direction of home even if there is no possibility of its returning. The Edible Snail, **Helix pomatia**, has been claimed to be able to orientate toward home at distances of up to 150–2000 m, yet it is unlikely that the animals would succeed in homing from such a distance (Edelstam and Palmer 1950).

Vanishing point and orientation cage data usually produce a scatter of individual directional preferences as shown in Fig. 3.4. Given such data, the experimenter is faced with a number of questions: (1) is there a directional preference or are the results due to chance; (2) if there is a directional preference, is it near enough to the home direction to be considered homeward orientation or is any similarity due to chance; and (3) given experimental treatment, is the performance of the experimental group significantly different from that of the untreated controls? There is a whole set of statistics, usually referred to as circular statistics, designed to answer such questions and detailed treatments may be found in Batschelet (1965, 1972, 1978). A summary of the statistics used in later chapters is presented in this book in Appendix 2. Briefly, however, treatment of the data involves the calculation of the **mean vector** for a given set of directional estimates (Fig. 3.4). This vector

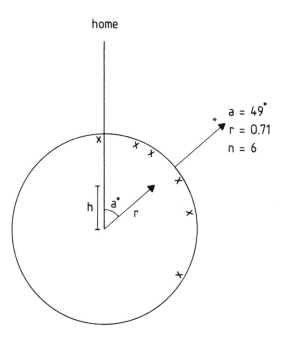

home

a = 49°
r = 0.71
n = 6

Fig. 3.4 Circular statistics and the graphical conventions used in this book
Method of calculating a°, r, and h is presented in Appendix 2.

The vertical line indicates the direction to be estimated by the experimental
subjects. In the diagram it is the direction of home, but it could be some other
such as geographical north or perhaps the direction of travel. Each cross is an
*individual's estimate of home direction (n = 6). The **mean vector** for these six*
estimates is represented by the oblique line. The mean vector has angle a° and
length r. If all estimates are in precisely the same direction, r = 1. If the
estimates are distributed uniformly around 360°, r = 0. The distribution of the
estimates is significantly non-uniform if r is significantly greater than 0 (see
Appendix 2). The vertical line outside the circle shows the mean vector if all
estimates are precisely in the home direction. The oblique lines inside and outside
the circle show the mean vector as calculated for the six crosses. The asterisk
indicates that the distribution of crosses is significantly non-uniform (* P<0·05;
** P<0·01). Comparison of the two lines outside the circle gives a visual
indication of the accuracy and consistency of the group's estimate of the home
*direction. h is the **homeward component** of the mean vector. When a = 0°,*
h = r. When all estimates are in precisely the home direction, h = 1·0. When all
estimates are in precisely the opposite direction, h = − 1·0. When the distri-
bution is uniform or when the mean angle is at right angles to the home direction,
h = 0·0.

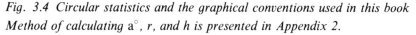

has both mean angle (a°) and length (r), the latter reflecting the amount of bias
toward the mean angle.

Orientation cage data, which always involve an individual 'pointing' in a variety of directions, are usually analysed in two stages (Batschelet 1978). A first-order analysis is carried out, involving calculation of the mean vector ($a°$, r) for each individual. These mean vectors are then subjected to second-order analysis for the group as a whole. This second-order analysis of mean vectors may involve only the mean angles ($a°$-values), or the lengths (r-values), or the two combined.

Although statistically it is possible to decide whether a first- or second-order mean angle is significantly different from the home direction, this statistic is rarely used in navigation research. There are two major reasons for this. First, animals do not always take the shortest route home from the release site. Homing Pigeons, for example, from some release sites show the greatest homing success when they leave the site at an angle many degrees (e.g. up to $60°$ or so) from the direct route to home (Keeton 1981). A set of vanishing points with a mean angle $30°$ or so and significantly different from the home direction does not necessarily mean, therefore, that the birds are unable to navigate. On the contrary, it may, on occasion, mean they are aware when the straightest route home is not the most economical.

Another situation in which a mean direction statistically different from the home direction may not reflect an inability to navigate is shown in Fig. 3.5. The experiment illustrated shows two features. First, the navigational accuracy of the rodents concerned varies with distance. Secondly, at all distances there is a consistent clockwise bias to the observed directional preferences relative to the direction of the assumed goal. This clockwise bias was unexplained. Similar consistent but as yet unexplained biases have been found in Homing Pigeons (Wallraff 1978) and, as shown later, in humans.

To somebody approaching the study of navigation for the first time, this statistical lenience probably looks extremely suspicious. If a mean direction significantly different from that of the assumed goal is not evidence against navigation from a particular release point, what is to stop an experimenter from claiming to have demonstrated navigation whatever mean direction is shown by his animals? The answer is that the true test for navigation is to carry out releases in at least two different and opposite directions from the assumed goal. Given data at all release directions that are significantly non-uniform (Fig. 3.4) and mean directions that are roughly homeward, an ability to navigate at the distances tested can be assumed, even if at some releases the mean direction is statistically different from the home direction (e.g. Fig. 3.6).

The shift in emphasis from homing success to ability to recognise home direction at the release point is fortuitous as far as the design of experiments on human navigation is concerned. The number of volunteers to take part in such experiments may have been somewhat reduced if the data needed were on homing success after release tens or hundreds of kilometres from home. As it is, humans can be asked to do essentially the same as animals tested in an orientation cage; that is to point towards home or to write down its compass bearing (e.g. N, NE, NNE, etc.). These estimates can then be subjected to the same analyses as orientation-cage or vanishing-point data for other animals.

Three series of displacement–release experiments on humans in which the subjects were blindfolded during the outward journey have now been carried out and reference to these is made at intervals throughout this book.

Series I was based on Manchester University and the surrounding area

distance from   trap direction

home   *P < 0.05   **P < 0.01

(m)

0-5   a = 86°
                                            r = 0.78

6-20   a = 43°
                                            r = 0.75

21-40   a = 22°
                                            r = 0.83

41-60   a = 25°
                                            r = 0.55

61-80   a = 41°
                                            r = 0.62

81 +   a = 95°
                                            r = 0.37

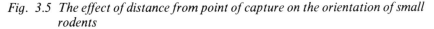

Fig. 3.5 The effect of distance from point of capture on the orientation of small rodents

The main experimental species was the European wood mouse, Apodemus sylvaticus. *Each dot is the mean angle for an individual as recorded in the orientation cage shown in Fig. 3.3. At all distances the second-order mean angles are measured clockwise from the home direction.*

(Simplified from Mather and Baker 1980)

(Baker 1980). Each October and November from 1976 to 1978, groups of 5–11 students were displaced, always in the afternoon, to release points between 6 and 52 km from the University (Fig. 3.7). The vehicle used was a Sherpa van (Fig. 3.9) with side windows and two long wooden bench seats such that the subjects sat facing at right angles to the direction of travel. The subjects were zoology and biology students between 20 and 22 years of age, all of whom had

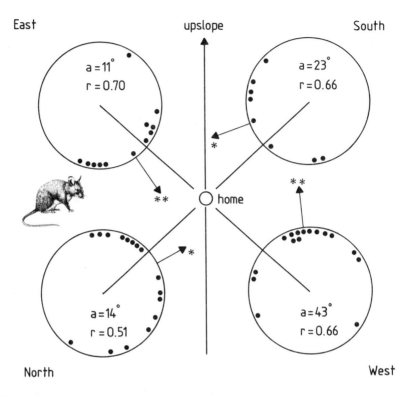

Fig. 3.6 A demonstration of goal orientation by small rodents

Rodents, mainly the European wood mouse, Apodemus sylvaticus, *were tested in an orientation cage in four different compass quadrants relative to point of capture. All mean angles are within 45° of home and are non-uniform, thus demonstrating goal orientation rather than simple orientation (e.g. upslope).*

(Re-drawn from Mather and Baker 1980)

lived in Manchester for at least 2 years. They had not specifically volunteered to take part in the experiment but had elected to study a third-year course in behavioural ecology for which the navigation exercise was a semi-compulsory part. The experiment began with the students being taken onto a University roof (Fig. 3.8) from which they could obtain a bird's-eye view of the distant horizon. After a few minutes they walked to a nearby car park where they climbed aboard the Sherpa and donned blindfolds. They were requested not to talk during the outward journey which was relatively tortuous (Fig. 3.7), more so than for most pigeon navigation experiments. Upon arrival, the students were removed individually through the Sherpa's rear doors. First, the subject was asked, out of earshot of other students, to state the compass direction (N, NNE, NE, etc.) of the release site from the University. The subject was then asked to point toward the University (Fig. 3.9) and the compass bearing measured to the nearest degree with a magnetic compass. Finally, the subject was asked to remove the blindfold and was allowed up to 2

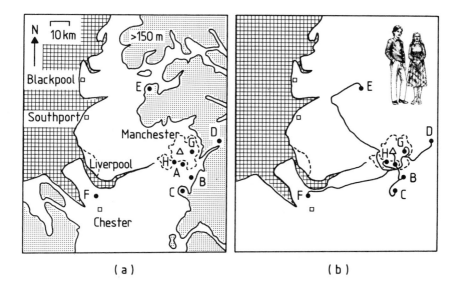

Fig. 3.7 Release sites and routes for Manchester (Series I) experiments on humans

(a) Release sites
Δ, Manchester University; ● A-H, release sites; stippled area, high ground;
(b) Displacement routes
All journeys began with a stage 8 km to the SSE.

minutes to reassess location before again pointing toward the University. The time taken to reach a decision was measured with a stop-watch. After making the visual estimate, the subject was asked to describe verbally the cues used to reach the various decisions. All release sites were chosen for an open aspect with a reasonable view (on a clear day) of the distant horizon (approximately 30 km). The tall buildings of Manchester City Centre were never visible, being either below the horizon or masked by strategically placed trees or buildings. Non-topographical clues such as signposts or passing buses, were also avoided. Visibility, wind speed and direction, and the conspicuousness of the sun's disc were recorded, both while on the University roof and at the release site, as was the proportion of the outward journey that the sun was shining.

Series II was carried out on 29 June 1979 at the suggestion and under the supervision of Yorkshire TV (Baker 1980). The location, subjects and equipment were all provided by the television company and were unfamiliar to the experimenter. The site chosen was Barnard Castle, County Durham, England and the subjects were sixth-form pupils aged 16–17 years from two local schools. In this series there was no preliminary visit to a roof but the subjects were told before the experiment began the direction of north, south, east and west. As group size was much larger (up to 42), displacement was carried out on board a coach similar to that shown in Fig. 3.10. Window-

*Fig. 3.8 All Series I and III experiments began with a visit to the Zoology
         Department roof*

(Photo by Les Lockey)

blinds were available and used for all of the windows but the rear.
Nevertheless, when the sun shone, its heat could still be felt on the face. In this
series, instead of stating their estimate of direction, the subjects were asked,
again while still blindfold, to write down their estimate of the compass direction of the release site from 'home' (i.e. school). Before the experiment began,
each individual had written their name and sex on the card provided. For the
sake of the television cameras, the subjects were removed from the coach *en
masse* before being asked to point toward home, first while still blindfold and
then with the blindfolds removed. However, the general chaos and extent of
the 'social interaction' that followed made these estimates unusable and from
series II only the written estimates are used.

Series III was based on Manchester University. Experimental design and
subjects were as for Series I except that group size was between 29 and 32 and
displacement was by coach (Fig. 3.10). As a result, subjects faced the direction
of travel. Four journeys were made at weekly intervals from 15 October to 5
November 1979. On the first journey, thick curtains covered all windows but
on the last three journeys the windows were uncovered. The major difference
between Series I and III, however, apart from the experimental treatments
(Chapter 6) was that the subjects were asked at a succession of sites during the

*Fig. 3.9 At the release site students were removed from the vehicle and asked
to point in the direction of the University, first while still blindfold, then
with the blindfold removed. Direction of pointing was recorded by the
experimenter, using a magnetic compass. Doors of the Sherpa van used
in Series I experiments have been left open to show seating
arrangement. Normally the doors would be closed while a subject was
being processed, usually about 10 m from the van.*

(Photo by Geoff. Thompson)

outward journey to write down not only their estimate of direction but also
the air-line distance of home. This technique permitted reconstruction of each
individual's estimate of the outward journey (e.g. Fig. 3.11).

Over the course of 16 journeys during the three series, there have been 43
release occasions using 33 different sites (Table 3.1). In all, 940 individual
releases have been achieved involving 140 different individuals of which 59
were females.

So far, this book has concentrated on designing experiments simply to
demonstrate the existence of navigational ability. Having done so, interest
shifts to the navigation mechanisms themselves. The next chapter outlines
some of the major principles.

Fig. 3.10 In Series II and III experiments, displacement was by coach (Photo by Les Lockey)

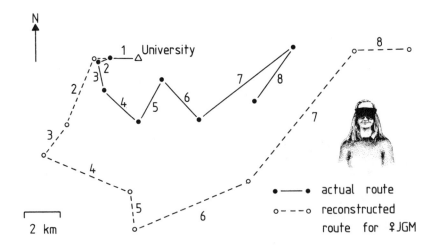

Fig. 3.11 Comparison of actual and estimated routes

In Series III, subjects were asked at several points during the outward journey to estimate direction and air-line distance from the University. These data allow each individual's estimate of the route to be reconstructed. Estimated and actual directions of each leg (numbered) of the journey and angle of turn between legs can thus be compared.

Table 3.1 Detailed breakdown of human navigation experiments

	Journeys	No. of release		Individuals			Individual	Reference
		Sites	Occasions	♂	♀	total	releases	
Series I								
Manchester	10	8	18	36	28	64	145	Baker 1980
Series II								
Barnard Castle	2	3	3	26	16	42	104	Baker 1980
Series III								
Manchester	4	22	22	19	15	34	691	In prep.
Total	16	33	43	81	59	140	940	

4

How to navigate

Figure 4.1 shows again the outward journey of a displacement experiment and the straight line direction from the release site to home that the experimenter assumes his subjects are trying to estimate. The mechanisms available to the subjects fall into two major categories: (1) **route-based navigation**; and (2) **location-based navigation**.

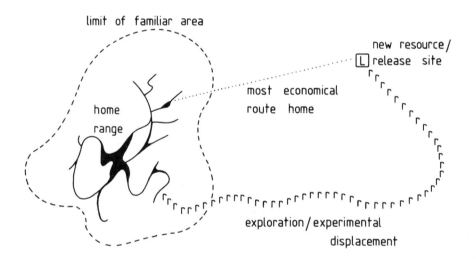

rrrr: route – based navigation   L: location – based navigation

Fig. 4.1 Route-based and location-based navigation in both natural exploration and experimental displacement

Route-based navigation is any mechanism of estimating home direction that results from the subject monitoring the outward route. Retracing precisely the outward journey is one form of route-based navigation (or perhaps, more appropriately, pilotage). This is the principle of Ariadne's thread. In Greek mythology is the story of Theseus who went to Crete to slay the Minotaur, a monster that lived in a labyrinth. Ariadne, a daughter of Minos, King of Crete, fell in love with Theseus and as he entered the labyrinth gave him a ball of thread so that he could find his way out. Theseus killed the Minotaur, successfully found his way out of the labyrinth, and fled from Crete with Ariadne, only to desert her on the Isle of Naxos.

The principle of Ariadne's thread is an important element in exploration and navigation, not only by humans. In this chapter, however, we are more concerned with mechanisms of monitoring the outward journey that allow the subject to estimate the dotted line in Fig. 4.1. The simplest method, of course, is to use familiar landmarks. If, at some stage during the outward journey, a landmark is passed that can be recognised as one perceivable from the home site, the animal can make use of the information. For example, if the last familiar landmark passed during the outward journey is known to be north of the home, the subject can travel roughly in the homeward direction by going south upon release, unless, of course, the direction of the outward journey changes considerably after passing that point.

As humans, we tend to think of landmarks as visual, topographical features, but they need not be. If a particularly recognisable smell is only detected at the home site when the wind is from the northeast, detection of that smell during the outward journey provides useful information, provided the current wind direction is known (Fig. 4.2). Acoustic landmarks are another possibility, if recognisable sounds come from a particular direction at the home site.

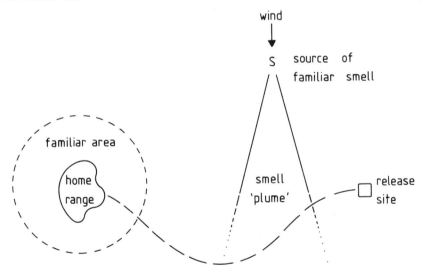

Fig. 4.2 The use of olfactory landmarks in route-based navigation

A recognisable smell from source S is detected by an animal in its home range only when the wind is from the northeast. If the smell is detected during experimental displacement on a day that the wind is from the north, it follows that the displacement route is somewhere between northeast and southeast of home.

A more efficient system of route-based navigation, in that it provides information right up to the moment of release and is not dependent on the outward journey passing near to familiar landmarks, is that of monitoring the compass direction of the different stages or 'legs' of the outward journey. If the speed and duration of each leg is also monitored, the whole can be integrated to produce a single vector which is the direction of home. To take a simple example, if the outward journey consists of one leg of 5 minutes duration to the northwest that is travelled twice as fast as a second 10 minute leg to the northeast, it follows that home direction from the release site is due south. An alternative is continuously to update estimated position so that the current direction of home is known throughout the outward journey. Either mechanism ideally requires the experimental subject to be able to measure the direction, speed and duration of travel. This may seem difficult for any animal, perhaps to the point of being impossible. Speed, however, could be dropped from the calculation if the animal 'assumed' rate of displacement was constant, and the effect on accuracy of slight variations would not be too severe. Time can be measured, using an internal clock, to within 0·3 per cent by many animals (Rawson, in Barlow 1964). The remaining requirement is an ability to monitor the direction of displacement. Essentially, this involves continuous, or at least frequent, detection of a cue such as the sun, stars, moon, or Earth's magnetic field.

All of the mechanisms for route-based navigation mentioned so far have involved the animal being able to refer to some external cue during displacement. There is an alternative mechanism that requires reference to internal cues. This is the system of inertial navigation found in modern jet planes and developed as a model for animal navigation by Barlow (1964). If an animal has some internal gyroscope system, such as the inner ear of vertebrates, it can detect all the twists and turns of the outward journey. If it can then integrate these with time spent travelling in straight lines it can theoretically produce an estimate of the current direction of home which can be continuously updated.

There seems no shortage of potential mechanisms by which an animal could carry out route-based navigation during displacement (or exploration). Experimentation involves selective reduction of the variety of cues available during the outward journey. Visual cues can be eliminated by using blindfolds. Magnetic cues can be manipulated by transporting animals in either a null or rotated artificial magnetic field. Olfactory cues can be masked by exposing the animals to more potent smells or by temporary deadening of the olfactory sense through the use of nasal anaesthetic sprays. Inertial cues can be masked by rotating the animals on turntables during displacement, and so on. There is, however, a major complication to the study of route-based navigation which results from its interaction with location-based navigation.

Location-based navigation can be either an alternative or a complement to route-based navigation. Any features of the environment by which an animal can recognise the direction of the release site from the home site can be used for location-based navigation. Before the possible mechanisms can be discussed, however, the difference has to be emphasised between an animal's familiar area and its **familiar-area map**. The familiar area is the sum of all those places an individual has visited before and can recognise. Surrounding

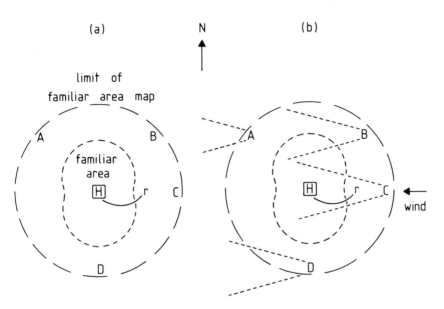

Fig. 4.3 The use in location-based navigation of distant visual and olfactory landmarks on the familiar area map

(a) Use of distant visual landmarks
A−D are distant landmarks that can be seen from the limits of the familiar area. From these limits, A is northwest, B is northeast, C is east, and D is south. When displaced to release site r, the apparent compass directions of the landmarks have changed. C is still east, but nearer. B is nearly due north; D is southwest. It follows that H lies to the west.

(b) Use of distant smells
A−D are sources of familiar smells. At H they are detected respectively with northwest, northeast, east and south winds. On the day of displacement the wind is from the east. The downwind plumes of the four smells are shown. At r, only smell C can be detected, more strongly than from H. It follows that H lies to the west.

(a) Simplified from Baker 1978; (b) Simplified from Papi 1976

the familiar area is a further zone, often very large, that previously has been perceived only from a distance. For example, when a human visits a village, this becomes part of his familiar area. At the same time, the mountains visible to the east of the village become part of his familiar-area map and can be used for location-based navigation (Fig. 4.3). For example, if in future the individual were ever to find himself in an unknown location but to the north of which the same mountains were visible, it would follow that the village was situated roughly to the northwest.

A familiar-area map consists of familiar landmarks and their spatial relationships. Such landmarks, as in route-based navigation, do not have to be visual. Any feature of the environment that is specific to a particular location can be used in location-based navigation, whether it is a mountain, a smell, a sound, a magnetic anomaly, or any other.

All of the mechanisms of location-based navigation so far have been based on familiar landmarks. Reliance on such mechanisms would limit the distance over which location-based navigation is possible to the furthest point from which familiar landmarks can be perceived. One of the burning questions in animal navigation is whether any animal (apart from humans *with* instruments) can perform location-based navigation from beyond the limits of their familiar-area map. So far, it has only seriously been suggested to be possible for birds and bats. The proposed mechanism is reference to some form of **grid map** comparable to the system of latitude and longitude used by humans with suitable instruments. In order to have access to a grid map, an animal has to perceive two features of the environment that each provide a geographic coordinate. A variety of possible features have been suggested, the most realistic of which are celestial cues and the Earth's magnetic field. Other less likely possibilities are discussed by Matthews (1968).

The best known of all grid maps so far suggested is that based on the daily arc of the sun (Matthews 1955). If an animal can measure both the sun's altitude and how far along its arc it has travelled, and can compare these measures at the release site with the measures that would have prevailed at the home site, it is a relatively simple matter to determine the direction of home (Fig. 4.4). Similar grid maps could be available at night, though the measurement of time would be more complex, from the arc of the moon or of individual stars. An alternative or complementary grid could also be derived

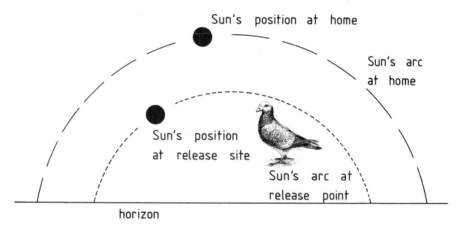

Fig. 4.4 The major elements of Matthews' sun-arc grid-map hypothesis

A displaced and released bird observes the sun's position at the release site and compares this with the position the sun would be in if the bird were at home. If the sun is lower than it should be, the release site is further from the equator than is home. If the sun has travelled less far along its daily arc than at home (i.e. local time is lagging behind home time) the release site is further west than is home. In the diagram, the release point, if in the northern hemisphere, is northwest of home.

from the Earth's magnetic field (Viguier 1882). The best map would be obtained from the inclination (the angle which lines of force make to the horizontal) and declination (the angle between magnetic and geographical north) of the Earth's field.

Students of birds, frustrated by an inability to find evidence for any grid map, have turned their attention to the possibility that animals may make use of environmental gradients. If an animal can detect the direction and slope of an environmental gradient over a short distance, it could then extrapolate the gradient to be useful for navigation from much greater distances beyond the limits of the animal's familiar-area map (Wiltschko and Wiltschko 1978). Proponents of such a navigational mechanism are still searching for suitable environmental features and detailed models have not yet been developed.

The study of location-based navigation requires careful design of experiments and particularly a knowledge of individual histories that for most animals is not usually available. Of major importance is a knowledge of whether the release point is within the animal's familiar area, beyond its familiar area but within its familiar-area map, or beyond both. Within its familiar area an animal is likely to respond by pilotage. Within its familiar-area map, it is likely to respond by location-based navigation involving landmarks. Beyond the familiar-area map the animal can employ location-based navigation only by reference to a grid map or to gradients.

It is relatively easy from this brief consideration of possible navigational methods, to see the objectives in experiments designed to study either route-based or location-based navigation. Unfortunately, experimentation is confounded by the interaction between the two. There are only two ways to separate the two methods. On the one hand an attempt can be made to remove all possibility of the animal's using one of the methods. Results should then relate only to the other. On the other hand, the animal can be tested for homeward orientation twice, once at the end of the outward journey but before it can perceive any feature of the release site, and then again after it has perceived its release site. Any improvement of the latter over the former can be attributed to location-based navigation.

The latter technique can easily be incorporated into the design of experiments on humans but for most animals neither technique has yet proved possible. As we shall see in the next few chapters, it has not yet been possible to unravel in any detail the interaction between route-based and location-based navigation for any non-human animal. The intriguing possibility gains strength, therefore, that experiments on humans may give insight into this interaction that will help enormously in the study of the navigation of other animals.

5

Route-based navigation: from fiction to fact

There is a ploy much favoured by the writers of detective and spy stories in which they contrive to have their hero captured, blindfolded, bundled into a car, and taken by a tortuous route to some secret refuge. Some time later the hero manages to track down the kidnappers by reconstructing his blindfold journey. Nor, in fiction, is this ability confined to males. In Arthur Hailey's *The moneychangers* (Hailey 1975), for example, Juanita Núñez is kidnapped, blindfolded and taken by car to a house for interrogation. After telling her captors what they want, she is again blindfolded, driven away from the house, and dumped. As soon as she is picked up by the police, she refuses to speak, demands pencil and paper, and immediately sets about reconstructing her second journey. Juanita Núñez, however, is no ordinary woman, but one with an exceptional memory.

Writers of fiction, therefore, allow that extraordinary individuals among humans are capable of solving the complex problems involved in route-based navigation when deprived of sight. Most people, however, would probably not expect to perform well in such a situation.

In navigation experiments, zoologists treat their non-human captives in the same way that fictional kidnappers treat theirs. Until recently, however, the possibility of route-based navigation received relatively little attention, having been surrounded by an aura of improbability. Only over the past decade has acceptance that route-based navigation by non-human animals is a reality gained momentum and the ability become a major subject for study. Since then, wherever the ability has been sought amongst navigating animals, some indication has eventually been found.

It is, of course, no surprise to find that when animals can control their own outward track, as during natural exploration, they can collect and use information about that track. Honey Bees, **Apis mellifera**, for example, when exploring for a new food source, collect information during their outward journey concerning both direction and distance. They later use this information to announce the location of the site to other individuals (Frisch 1967). Rather, the surprise comes when it is found that animals can still carry out route-based navigation even during artificial displacement and even when deprived of their more important senses. The range of definite examples is still small, but implications may be found for even the most unexpected animals. For example, when Edible Snails, **Helix pomatia**, are displaced in a cloth bag in autumn, they are able to orientate toward their winter home range from distances of up to at least 40 m. Indeed, all traces of homeward orientation do not disappear until displacement distances between 150 and 2000 m (Edelstam and Palmer 1950). The navigational mechanisms have never been demonstrated though route-based navigation may be involved. If the bag is shaken during displacement, homeward orientation upon release disappears. In this case, however, it is always possible that such rough treatment reduces motivation to home (Baker 1978) rather than ability for route-based navigation.

Amphibians displaced in open containers orient upon release in the compass direction opposite to the direction of displacement (Ferguson 1971). If only part of the displacement is in open containers with the sun visible, orientation upon release is opposite to the direction of displacement during that leg. The animals take no account of the displacement direction during the leg that the sun was not visible. Finally, when displaced in light-tight containers, there is no immediate homeward orientation upon release, though this may appear later. If conditions during displacement influence orientation upon release, it is a reasonable inference that route-based navigation is being used.

Orientation cage experiments on rodent navigation have demonstrated an ability to orient towards home at distances of up to 2–3·7 km before the animals can see their surroundings at the release site (Lindenlaub 1955, Bovet 1960, Fisler 1967). Mather and Baker (1980) displaced Wood Mice, **Apodemus sylvaticus**, and tested them before the mice were allowed to see their surroundings and, at the same time, while they had much reduced olfactory information, though 'local' air at the release site was probably not totally excluded. A similar indication of homeward orientation was found (Fig. 5.1). Again, the results suggest, but do not prove, that rodents may be capable of route-based navigation even when deprived of vision during displacement.

The only convincing evidence comes, as might be expected, from studies on Homing Pigeons. Moreover, it comes from two different lines of study. First, when pigeons are taken to a common release site by two different routes, it is often found that their vanishing points differ in accordance with the routes taken. Usually, such detour experiments produce results which suggest that the pigeons give greatest weight to the first stage of their outward journey (Fig. 5.2). Secondly, the crates or boxes in which the pigeons are housed during displacement also influence their ability to orient toward the home loft. Birds displaced in aluminium containers produce vanishing points with a bias in the home direction whereas birds displaced in iron containers do not (Papi *et al.* 1978).

It seems, therefore, that Homing Pigeons and perhaps a variety of other animals are able, even when deprived of their major sense, to perform route-based navigation to an accuracy rivalling the best heroes and heroines of fiction. Are these animals exceptional or is such an ability shared by all species that explore and navigate? In particular, are real humans, like those of fiction, also capable of such navigation?

The route-based mechanisms of navigation used by different races of humans when they explore by a route under their own control are considered in Chapter 8. Unless exploration is to traverse large areas of featureless sea, snow or desert, it is not too difficult to collect visual information that subsequently can be used for navigation back to the familiar area. Route-

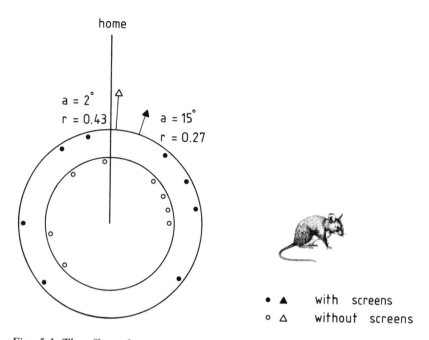

home

a = 2°
r = 0.43

a = 15°
r = 0.27

• ▲ with screens
○ △ without screens

Fig. 5.1 The effect of an opaque screen on the orientation of European Wood mice, Apodemus sylvaticus, *following displacement/release*

Wood mice were displaced and, without being allowed to see their surroundings during transfer, were tested in an orientation cage surrounded by an opaque screen. They could see the sky but not vegetation. There seemed to be a marginal improvement in homeward orientation when the screens were removed, suggesting the use of visual cues, but an indication of homeward orientation even when the screens were in position. This could have been due to route-based navigation or perhaps to location-based navigation using non-visual cues. Each dot is the mean vector for one individual mouse.
(Drawn from data collected by Mather and Baker)

based navigation under such normal circumstances can be taken for granted and to one degree or other is probably within everybody's personal experience. The question of interest in this chapter is the extent to which the outward journey can be removed from a person's control and the available information reduced without destroying navigational ability. In particular, in the absence of vision, which senses emerge as the most important?

In an experiment carried out in a flat, open yard, Worchel (1951) led blindfolded subjects along two sides of an isosceles triangle and then asked them to return to the starting point unaided by completing the triangle. When the hypoteneuse length was 2·46 m, the mean distance between estimated and real starting points was 0·74 ±0·34(s.d.) m; when 6·77 m, the mean distance was 2·28 ±1·32 m. Lindberg and Gärling (1978) led blindfolded subjects for 100 m or so through culverts beneath the University Hospital of Umeå. The paths taken had, with one exception, 90° angles of turn and were approxi-

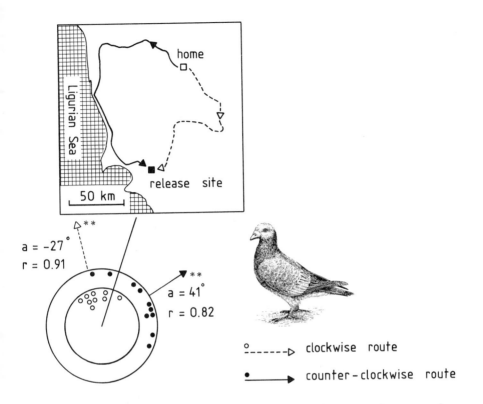

Fig. 5.2 The demonstration of route-based navigation by pigeons by means of a detour experiment

When pigeons are displaced to a common release point by two different routes, initial orientation upon release reflects the direction of the first stage of the journey. Solid dots relate to solid route. Open dots relate to dashed route. (Modified from Papi 1976)

mately level throughout. At each stop, the subject was told by the experimenter to estimate direction and air-line distance to the starting point. The results were not analysed by circular statistics but suggested a reasonable accuracy at judging direction and a tendency to underestimate distance. Evidently some ability for route-based navigation exists over distances of a few to a few tens of metres; what about longer distances?

Figure 5.3 summarises the verbal and written estimates of home direction obtained during the Series I and II displacement–release experiments (Chapter 3). The evidence seems overwhelming. Even when blindfold, humans show a capacity for route-based navigation over journeys of tens of kilometres. The writers of fiction, therefore, were correct in their supposition that such a feat is possible; but incorrect in their implication that only the extraordinary amongst us are capable of such a feat. The ability seems to be present in most people, at least among the age groups and social classes tested.

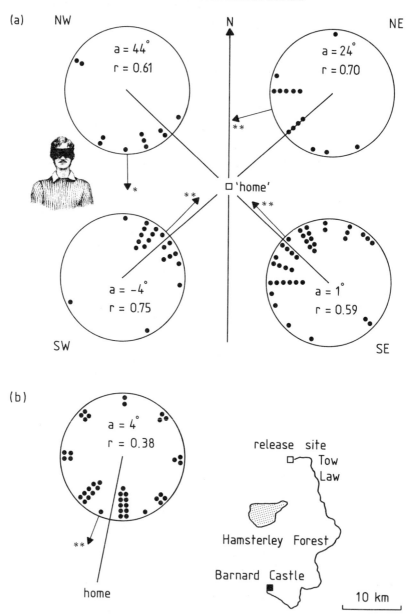

Fig. 5.3 A demonstration of route-based navigation by humans

a) Series I experiments, Manchester
b) Series II experiment, Barnard Castle

Each dot is one individual's verbal (Series I) or written (Series II) estimate of home direction while still blindfolded. In (a) data are lumped for all releases in each compass quadrant relative to 'home'.
(Re-drawn from Baker 1980)

No comparable experiments have been carried out on hunter–gatherers, pastoralists, or agriculturalists, though there is one historical record of particular interest. It concerns Tupaia, a dispossessed high chief and navigator from Raiatea, about 150 km westnorthwest of Tahiti in the Pacific. Tupaia was encountered by Captain James Cook and accompanied the Captain on board the *Endeavor* to Batavia, a distance of nearly 10 000 km. Despite the distance involved and despite the ship's circuitous route between 48° south latitude and 4° north, Tupaia was able to point toward Tahiti at any position throughout the journey (Forster 1778). This ability to point towards home, or toward any other familiar but invisible island beyond the horizon, is a major feature of Polynesian exploration and navigation and is discussed in Chapter 8.

Demonstration of an ability for route-based navigation in Man and other animals is only the first step. The real question of interest concerns the mechanisms on which the ability is based. Writers of fiction often guess how route-based navigation could be carried out. Arthur Hailey, for example, in *The moneychangers*, has Juanita Núñez scribble notes, seven handwritten pages in all, describing in detail the car's journey as detected while blindfold and stored in her extraordinary memory. Her notes ran something like this: short reverse from garage; forward, 8 seconds; almost stop; turn left, 10 seconds, medium speed; turn right, 2 seconds; . . . ; turn right, long straight stretch, high speed, 68 seconds; curving to left . . . ; and so on.

Arthur Hailey's Juanita is perhaps typical of fictional navigators in that she opts to use inertial navigation and memorises the details of the journey in sequence, working on the principle of Ariadne's thread. Other writers prefer their characters to note particular smells or sounds: a brewery or fish dock; the sound of a railway yard or the striking of a particular clock. In the final analysis, real life is even more remarkable.

Early experiments on Homing Pigeons allowed for route-based navigation only in relation to inertial mechanisms. It is an old idea, mentioned by Charles Darwin (1873), that if a bird could record all turns and distances while being displaced it could determine the straight-line direction and distance from home. In recent times, development of the inertial navigation model owes most to Barlow (1964). Data for Homing Pigeons have been summarised by Matthews (1968) and Schmidt-Koenig (1979). At first sight, the evidence is overwhelmingly negative, though closer examination shows that none of it is absolutely critical.

Homing Pigeons have been subjected to a number of experiments designed to disrupt inertial navigation if it were to exist. Various authors have rotated birds on a turntable during displacement. Others have displaced the birds using wide detours or by aeroplane in strictly clockwise or anti-clockwise spirals. Yet others have displaced birds under anaesthesia or after surgical bisection of the semicircular canals and other parts of the vestibular apparatus of the inner ear assumed to be involved in inertial navigation, were it to exist. Apart from detour experiments, none of these techniques have given positive results, control and experimental birds producing similar data for vanishing points and homing success. As pointed out by Schmidt-Koenig (1979), however, consistent though this evidence may appear, in all cases there remains a loophole. The bird's inertial system may be sufficiently sensitive and accurate not to be upset by circuitous detours or turntables. Anaesthesia may not be deep enough to prevent the bird from monitoring the journey and surgery on one part of the inner ear still leaves the possibility that turns and acceleration may be detected by what remains or by some other system altogether, such as movements of the viscera (Delius and Emmerton 1978).

In addition to those noted by Schmidt-Koenig, there is one other fundamental difficulty in any attempt to demonstrate that a particular mechanism, not only inertial navigation, is used in route-based navigation. This arises from the interaction of route-based with location-based navigation. In all of the above experiments, the birds were released at sites and under conditions in which they could have used location-based navigation. Even if the experimental procedures had disrupted inertial navigation, and even if no other mechanisms for route-based navigation were available, the birds may still have oriented toward home by switching to this alternative mechanism of location-based navigation. As far as inertial navigation is concerned, therefore, the situation is as summarised by Schmidt-Koenig (1979): although the evidence is negative and although most experts agree that inertial navigation is unlikely to be a major factor in the route-based navigation of Homing Pigeons, the final convincing evidence to disprove the inertial navigation hypothesis has yet to be obtained.

The first really convincing demonstration of route-based navigation by pigeons came from the detour experiments carried out by Papi and his co-workers in Italy (Fig. 5.2). Subsequent detour experiments carried out by other workers in other countries (summarised by Schmidt-Koenig 1979) have more often than not also found some effect. However, a detour should only influence vanishing point directions if the birds give more weight to the first stage than to later stages of the outward journey. On occasions that this does not happen, detour experiments should have no effect even though route-based navigation still occurs.

Papi (1976) argued that when detour experiments produced an influence it was due to the birds' detecting familiar olfactory cues which became less common as distance from the home site increased. Experiments in which pigeons were prevented from sampling olfactory cues *en route* by displacing them with their nostrils plugged or in air-tight containers produced a significant effect on initial orientation. Experiments were also tried in which strong-smelling substances were applied on or near the birds' nostrils in an attempt to mask the cues being perceived. Again, significant effects were sometimes obtained. In general, experiments on the role of olfaction in route-based navigation by pigeons have produced consistently positive results in Italy but inconsistent or negative results in the United States and Germany (Schmidt-Koenig 1979). Although it seems clear that pigeons, like the heroes of spy stories, can use familiar smells to monitor their outward journey, this cannot be the only or even the major technique available to them. A much more general mechanism seems to be one based on reference to the Earth's magnetic field.

Papi *et al.* (1978) displaced pigeons in different containers, one of iron and one of aluminium, and found a difference in initial orientation that could be attributed to the altered magnetic field in the iron container. Similarly, Wiltschko and Wiltschko (1978) found that when they transported pigeons in a crate on top of the engine of their Volkswagen squareback, disturbed orientation was sometimes observed that could have been due to magnetic activity produced by the generator. Much more controlled experiments have been reported by Kiepenheuer (1978a,b), Wiltschko and Wiltschko (1978), and Wiltschko, Wiltschko and Keeton (1978). In these, the crates were surrounded by Helmholtz coils which were used during displacement to reverse either or both the horizontal or vertical components of the Earth's magnetic field. In different experiments, birds were either disoriented upon release or produced vanishing-point distributions clearly rotated relative to the controls (Fig. 5.4). The evidence seems convincing that during displacement pigeons sample geomagnetic information and make use of this in route-based navigation.

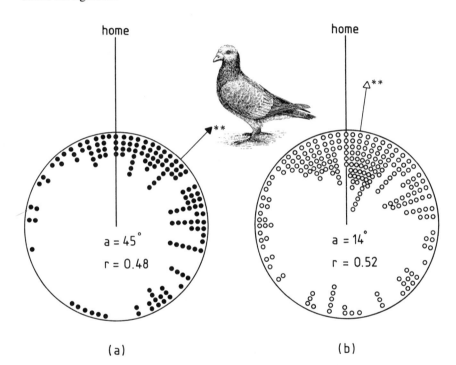

Fig. 5.4 Effect of a reversed vertical magnetic field during displacement on the initial orientation of pigeons upon release

(a) Experimental birds exposed to reversed field
(b) Control birds exposed to normal geomagnetic field
(Re-drawn from Kiepenheuer 1978a)

Pigeons, it seems, can go one better than the heroes of fiction. They have a sense, the magnetic sense, to which they can refer during their outward journey, backed up, whenever possible, by the detection of familiar olfactory landmarks. What senses and mechanisms are used by humans? Most attempts to answer this question in the past have been made using subjects displaced in confined spaces or, if outside, over short distances of a few metres.

A number of laboratory-type experiments have been carried out in which navigational ability is compared when subjects are moved passively and then allowed to move themselves. Liebig (in Howard and Templeton 1966) showed his subjects a light in an otherwise dark room. When the light was put out, the subjects were either led about or wheeled passively on a cart along paths of varying complexity. They then had to point to, and return to, the position of the light. Subjects who walked about performed more accurately than those who were wheeled. Beritoff (in Barlow 1964) carried out similar experiments, with similar results, on deaf-mute children (and dogs and cats).

Such results suggest a role in route-based navigation for **kinaesthesis** (i.e. discrimination of the positions and movements of body parts based on information other than visual, auditory or verbal—Howard and Templeton 1966). Kinaesthetic information comes from muscular contraction, the relative movements of parts of the body, and changes in length, tension and compression, etc. generated by the effects of gravity.

Useful though the kinaesthetic sense may be, it is not without its idiosyncrasies. It is well known that when people are lost in a mist, they commonly find they have walked in a complete circle, a fate that once befell Lord Baden Powell, founder of the scout movement (Gatty 1958). The most detailed study of this behaviour is perhaps that by Lund (1930) who asked his subjects to walk blindfolded in a straight line across a football field. Their track was plotted and consistent veering was found, most often to the right. When asked to walk backwards, the geographical direction of veering was reversed. Most subjects had a longer left leg and most of these veered to the right. Average difference in leg length was about 5 mm. This suggests, and most authors accept, that body asymmetry, not only of the legs, is the explanation for the tendency to veer, which also occurs when swimming or driving. Howard and Templeton (1966) suggested that vestibular asymmetry may also be involved.

Böök and Gärling (1978a, b) required subjects to carry out in a dark room either active body rotation (up to 75°) or linear locomotion and then to estimate the direction or distance respectively of a target lamp that had been visible before the experiment began. They found several differences in estimation of body rotation as compared to linear locomotion. First, subjects overcompensated for body rotation but undercompensated for linear locomotion. Secondly, if the target light remained on during displacement, subjects were more consistent at judging distance but not at judging angle. On the other hand, subjects with an invisible target overcompensated for body rotations increasingly as the angle increased. Evidently vision played some role, though a variable one, in the judgement of rotation and distance. Moreover, this role is not confined to the actual time of making the estimate. Past experience is also important. Worchel (1951), using the triangle completion task mentioned earlier, found that sighted subjects were more accurate than blind, even though both were blindfolded. Some other workers, though not all, have obtained similar results (see review by Howard and Templeton 1966). Those workers who found sighted subjects to be superior concluded that the availability of visual imagery facilitates the symbolisation of the patterns involved in the task. Additional support for this conclusion comes from further experiments which show that individuals blind at birth perform less well in later orientation tasks than individuals with some visual experience before blinding.

Although these experiments clearly show that vision, and perhaps visual imagery, assist the judgement of rotation and distance, they also show that it is not essential. Blind and blindfolded subjects, although in general not as able as sighted subjects, nevertheless show some ability at the different navigation tasks. In Beritoff's experiments on deaf-mute children (in Barlow 1964) only those with functional vestibular organs showed an ability for spatial orientation in a room. Dogs and cats with surgical impairment of their vestibular organs were also disoriented.

These experiments imply a critical involvement of the vestibular organs in judging turns and perhaps distances in confined spaces. In less confined spaces, however, vestibular function may not always be as essential. In a continuation of the isosceles triangle experiment in an open area, Worchel (1952) found that subjects with defective vestibular functions did no worse than those with high vestibular sensitivity. Worchel interpreted his results as indicating that persons with deficient vestibular sensitivity compensate by developing their kinaesthetic sensitivity. Whatever the explanation, the apparent difference in mechanisms in different tasks in different environments over different distances advises caution in extrapolating from short- to longer-distance experiments such as Series I to III of the displacement–release experiments carried out around Manchester and Barnard Castle.

On two occasions during Series I of these experiments on undergraduates the group was divided into two, half wearing blindfolds during the outward journey, the other half not. The results are presented in Fig. 5.5 and show that sighted individuals perform marginally better than those wearing blindfolds.

The sighted students in these experiments stated that they had relied largely on road signs and place names in monitoring their journey. The blindfolded students, however, in these as in all other experiments, could not describe in any convincing way how they had managed to monitor their journey. On days when the sun was shining during displacement, some claimed to have made use of the heat of the sun on the face as a directional clue. Others claimed to have tried to detect left and right turns and to relate them to a memorised map of the region. Most admitted, however, that they found this was possible only during the first few minutes of the journey and that they soon became lost. On occasion, also, some individuals claimed to have recognised (usually incorrectly) particular industrial smells associated with different parts of the Manchester region and others to have recognised particular sounds, such as aircraft coming in to land at Manchester airport. Yet others tried to detect when the van or coach started to climb or descend hills and to relate this to a knowledge of the topography of the region. The vast majority, however, considered themselves to be lost and their estimate of direction while still blindfold to be no more than a guess. The students were always genuinely surprised when their group estimate turned out to be as accurate as indicated in Fig. 5.3.

There is no doubt that all of the cues mentioned by the students could provide information useful for route-based navigation. The key question,

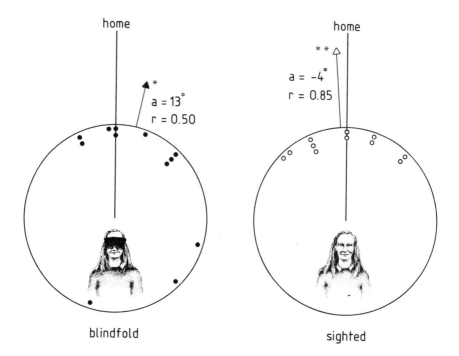

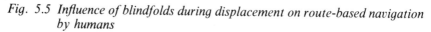

Fig. 5.5 Influence of blindfolds during displacement on route-based navigation by humans

On two journeys during Series I (to Sites G and H) half of the subjects were blindfolded, the remainder were allowed normal vision. Each dot is one individual's verbal estimate of home direction.

however, is whether these factors are sufficient to account for the level of route-based navigation actually observed. Two of the factors at least, the heat of the sun and familiarity with the route, can be evaluated from the data.

If the heat of the sun on the face is an essential cue, we should expect that accurate route-based navigation occurs only when the sun is shining throughout a major part of the outward journey. Figure 5.6 summarises all data for extreme conditions of sunshine during the outward journey. Although route-based navigation seems to be more reliable on days with long periods of sun, the ability does not disappear even on days of complete and heavy overcast. Indeed, the mean direction is nearer the home direction when the sun is not shining or when there are blinds or curtains over the windows. Evidently, therefore, perception of the sun's position relative to the direction of displacement is not the basis of route-based navigation, though it may be used when possible.

If memorised-map following were the key factor, the data would be expected to show two features. First, the accuracy of route-based navigation should decrease with increase in the release distance on the assumption that familiarity decreases with distance from the city centre. Secondly, individuals

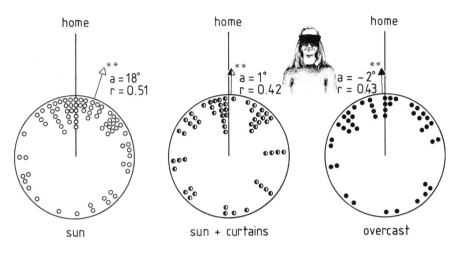

Fig. 5.6 The lack of influence of sunshine during displacement on the accuracy of route-based navigation by humans

Each dot is one individual's written or verbal estimate of home direction. Data from Series I, II, and III are lumped according to conditions during displacement. Three conditions are shown: continuous sunshine; sunshine but with curtains or blinds across the coach windows; and total overcast.

who, upon removal of their blindfold, find they are familiar with the release site, should produce better estimates of home direction while still blindfold than individuals who are not. The criterion used for familiarity in these tests was that the subject claimed to have visited the release site before and could name its location to within 2 km. Figure 5.7 shows that there is no clear decrease in accuracy of the stated blindfold estimates with increasing distance of release and that individuals familiar with the release site are no better at their route-based estimate than individuals that are not.

Further evidence that memorised-map following is not a key factor in route-based navigation is provided by Fig. 5.8. In Series III experiments the subjects were asked for written blindfold estimates during the outward journey at a succession of positions, the first of which was usually within 2 km of home. At this position, performance is relatively good but then rapidly decreases before once more improving as the journey progresses. This is consistent with the students' assertion that they could often follow their route as far as the first position but then became lost. It would seem, therefore, that memorised-map following is an initial element in navigation but is then abandoned in favour of some other method which is capable of restoring navigational ability despite a temporary phase of being lost.

The pattern shown in Fig. 5.8. suggests strongly that in the Manchester and Barnard Castle experiments the students are not using inertial navigation. If route-based navigation were dependent on inertial mechanisms, these would have to be continuous. Once lost, a sense of location cannot be restored. An

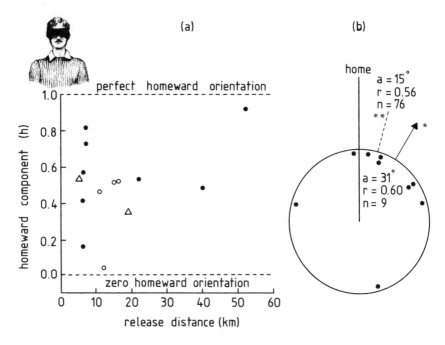

Fig. 5.7 *Two tests for the involvement of long-distance map following in route-based navigation by humans*

(a) *The effect of release distance*
If memorised-map following were an important mechanism, the accuracy of homeward orientation should decrease with distance. There is no indication that this occurs. Each dot shows the homeward component of written or verbal estimates made by groups at the final release point on each journey. ●, Series I releases; △, Series II; ○, Series III.

(b) *The influence of familiarity with the release site*
Each dot shows the verbal estimate of home direction (while still blindfolded) of subjects that, when the blindfold was removed, recognised where they were. Mean vector for these estimates is shown by the solid line. The dashed line shows the mean vector for individuals not familiar with the release site. If memorised map following were important, individuals familiar with the release site should perform better than those not. There is no indication that this is so. Data from Series I.

estimate 180° in error early on in displacement will remain at 180° even if all subsequent inertial navigation is accurate (Fig. 5.9). Figure 5.10 compares the change in accuracy as the journey progresses for individuals that within the first two positions during the journey are either very accurate (0 ±30°) or very inaccurate (180° ±30°) in their estimate of home direction. It can be seen that by the final position the difference between the two groups has virtually disappeared.

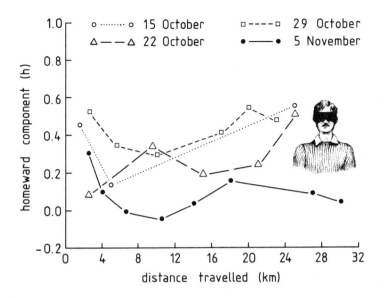

Fig. 5.8 Variation in homeward component with distance travelled during single journeys

Series III experiments allowed the subjects' estimates of the outward journey to be reconstructed (Fig. 3.11). Homeward component seems to begin high, decreases to a trough at 5–10 km, and thereafter gradually increases. From this it is suggested that memorised-map following occurs only during the first 3 km or so of the outward journey, eventually giving way to a different mechanism. The poor performance on 5 November was due entirely to males. Females were as well-oriented as on previous occasions (see Chapter 10).

Figures 5.8 and 5.10 show that the accuracy of route-based navigation cannot be attributed to inertial navigation. Nevertheless, many of the students claimed to have attempted to follow the right and left turns of the journey. In Series III, each individual's estimate of the outward journey could be reconstructed (Chapter 3). It was possible from these reconstructions to measure each individual's estimate of the angle between successive legs of the journey. These estimates could then be compared with the actual angles. Figure 5.11 suggests that some weak ability to measure these angles of turn may exist when the angle between successive legs is small. Changes in direction much greater than 90°, however, are grossly under- or over-estimated. This implies, however, that when the outward journey is relatively straight, a combination of memorised-map following over the first few kilometres and subsequent inertial navigation might be sufficient for reasonably accurate route-based navigation. With complex journeys as used in Series I to III, however, inertial navigation would seem to be of little use.

One feature of the experiments in Series II and III, in which displacement was by coach, was that during the journey some of the subjects fell asleep. This did not happen in Series I, presumably because conditions in the Sherpa van

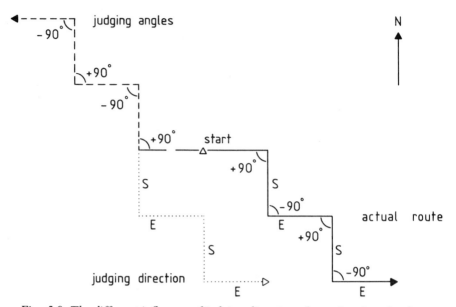

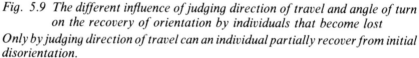

Fig. 5.9 The different influence of judging direction of travel and angle of turn on the recovery of orientation by individuals that become lost

Only by judging direction of travel can an individual partially recover from initial disorientation.

were so uncomfortable. Pigeons are also prone to sleep during displacement and in the past this fact has been considered a good indicator that route-based navigation is not taking place. In Series III experiments, subjects were asked to record any occasions that they fell asleep. Reconstruction of each individual's estimate of their outward journey in this series allowed retrospective measurement of not only the estimated angle between successive legs but also the estimated direction of each leg. Figure 5.12 compares the estimates of leg direction made by individuals while asleep and awake. Data are few but suggest that the ability to monitor direction disappears during sleep. At the same time, the figure suggests that the subjects most likely to sleep are also the least accurate at judging direction of travel. Nevertheless, by the end of the journey all errors had cancelled out and, despite having slept at some stage, these individuals were still able to produce a reasonable estimate of home direction.

There is no indication that the estimates of distance were any different for individuals that slept during some leg of the journeys. In general, all subjects overestimated air-line distance from home (Fig. 5.13). Similar over-estimations occur when subjects estimate distances travelled without blind-folds on trains (Canter 1977). Experiments in which subjects travel by their own locomotion, however, have resulted in underestimations of distance (Böök and Gärling 1978a, Lindberg and Gärling 1978). In Series III the indication is that subjects are estimating time travelled rather than distance (Fig. 5.13).

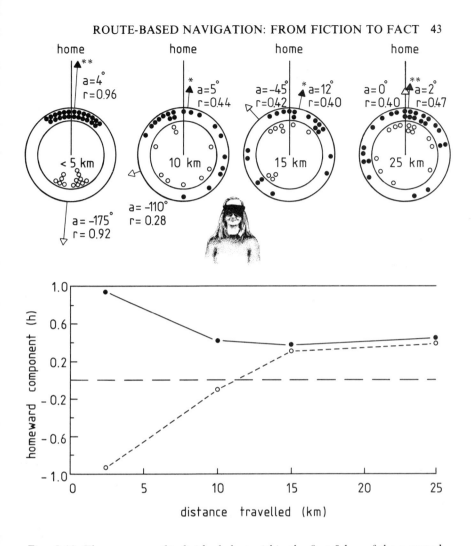

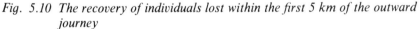

Fig. 5.10 The recovery of individuals lost within the first 5 km of the outward journey

●, *individuals accurate to within* ±30° *during the first 5 km;* ○, *individuals 180° ±30° in error during the same distance. Within the next 10 km of the journey the initially disoriented individuals have recovered nearly to match the orientation of those initially well-oriented. Data from Series III.*

So far, therefore, we have made little progress toward identifying the mechanism of route-based navigation by blindfolded humans over distances of tens of kilometres. Conscious mechanisms, such as reference to the sun and to occasional familiar smells and sounds, may sometimes assist but they are not the main mechanism. Nor is inertial navigation, which apparently plays little if any part unless the outward journey is relatively simple. Memorised-map following is useful only over the first few kilometres. Whatever the major

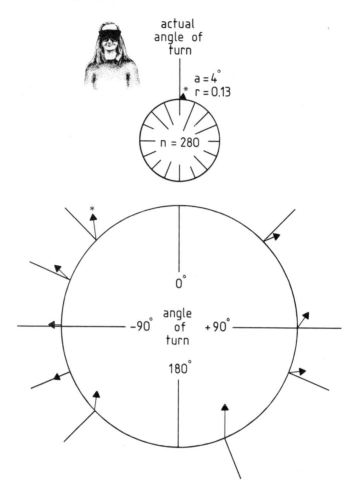

Fig. 5.11 Ability to measure angle of turn between successive legs of the outward journey is weak

Figure drawn from reconstructed outward journeys, Series III. In the lower diagram, lines without arrowheads show actual angles of turn and represent a mean vector of 0·5. Lines with arrowheads show mean vectors for estimates of different actual angles of turn. The greater the actual angle, the weaker the ability to estimate it accurately. The upper diagram lumps all estimates relative to actual angle of turn. Length of lines inside the circle indicates number of individuals making a particular estimate.

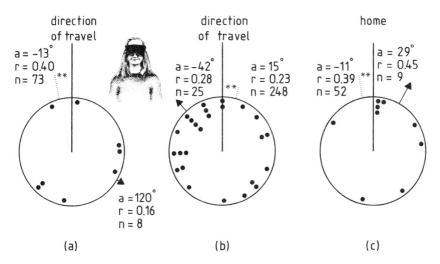

Fig. 5.12 Influence of sleep on ability to estimate direction of travel

Each dot shows an estimate of direction by an individual who claimed to have slept at some stage during the outward journey. While asleep (a), ability to estimate direction of travel disappears (solid arrowhead) compared with the ability of awake individuals to measure the direction of the same legs (dotted mean vector). In (b) ability to measure direction of travel while awake of individuals prone to sleep (solid mean vector) also seems weaker than the ability of other individuals during the same legs (dotted mean vector). In (c) the estimates of final position of those that slept at some stage during the outward journey is only marginally reduced as far as can be determined from the small sample size. Sample size in (c) is greater than in (a) because one individual noted that he had fallen asleep on one journey but failed to record during which leg.

mechanism may be, it seems to rest on a largely unconscious sense, to be lost during sleep, and to allow a sense of location to be regained after temporary disorientation. There seems to be only one remaining possibility: that, like pigeons, humans sample geomagnetic information during the outward journey. This astounding possibility is examined in the next chapter. It leads us into the realms of the sixth sense and instinctive pathfinding. Moreover, it leads us into speculations that many would consider inappropriate to serious scientists and into an area that has been a haven for many a charlatan. Nevertheless, it is an area into which we are directed by solid, zoological example. Whatever the repercussions, we have no alternative but to take seriously the possibility that Man has a magnetic sense of direction.

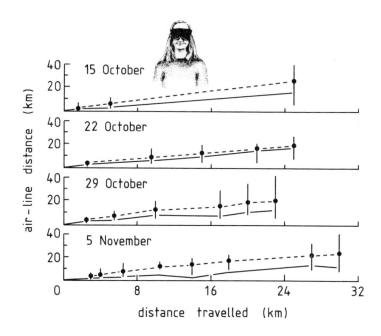

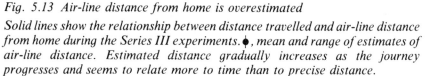

Fig. 5.13 Air-line distance from home is overestimated

Solid lines show the relationship between distance travelled and air-line distance from home during the Series III experiments. ♦, mean and range of estimates of air-line distance. Estimated distance gradually increases as the journey progresses and seems to relate more to time than to precise distance.

6

A new human sense: the compass in the head

The term 'sixth sense' was coined in 1905 by Emile Jarval (Gatty 1958). He concluded from the ability of blind people to find their way around and to avoid obstacles in their path that there had to be a sense additional to the five senses of conventional literature and philosophy—sight, hearing, smell, taste and touch. In fact, it is of course inappropriate to refer to this unknown sense as a 'sixth' sense. Man has many more senses (e.g. of time, balance, temperature) than the conventional five. Nevertheless, the term has stuck and for many people the, at first sight inexplicable, sense of direction apparently possessed by the blind and by non-industrialist peoples is attributable to a sixth sense.

Before Jarval and the sixth sense, the pathfinding ability of non-industrialists was discussed in terms of 'instinctive' direction finding. However, according to Gatty (1958) this line of thought only began in the middle of the last century. Earlier, in the ancient writings of both the orient and the west, such a concept does not exist. Responsibility for drawing attention to a mysterious sense of direction belongs largely to the uncritical testimony of a few nineteenth-century missionaries and explorers. A french missionary, Père François Xavier de Charlevois, produced strange theories and grossly exaggerated the supposedly instinctive pathfinding abilities of the Amerindians. Sir H. Bartle Frere, a one-time Governor of the region of Sind in India described the way that, in this flat region where there are neither natural landmarks nor tracks, the best guides rely on an 'infallible instinct' (Frere 1870). Finally, Wrangel (1840) in describing his expedition to Siberia in 1820–23, praised his Cossack driver's ability to maintain direction and wrote that he 'appeared to be guided by a kind of unerring instinct'. When, in 1873, *Nature* invited correspondence on the mysterious sense of direction of men and other animals, Charles Darwin misquoted Wrangel and said that the Cossacks *were* guided by instinct. These early writings and Darwin's misquotation were taken up and enlarged upon by later writers. The result was that throughout the latter part of the nineteenth century and much of the twentieth, non-industrialist humans, and some exceptional Europeans, were widely and generally considered to have a sixth sense for direction finding.

This readiness to accept the existence of a sixth sense prevailed in spite of observations that made such acceptance unnecessary (Gatty 1958). As early as 1724, the Jesuit missionary Père Joseph Lafitau had given a clear account of how the Iroquois Amerindians found their way through dense country entirely by visual means. Frere (1870) in describing pathfinding by the inhabitants of the Sind region of India, in the same breath as saying there were no natural landmarks, referred to the interminable succession of sand dunes all aligned with the direction of the prevailing wind of the south-west monsoon. In the same way, Wrangel, while mystified by his Cossack driver's sense of direction, noted the parallel ridges of snow, also aligned with the dominant winds. Such a directional cue had been used by the famous Antarctic explorer, Sir Douglas Mawson, in 1913 when, after being trapped for 36 hours by thick drift and an eighty kilometre per hour wind, was able to set out in the correct direction by orienting to the wind-blown show that had formed parallel ridges.

Various suggestions as to the basis of the sixth sense have been made, ranging from electricity and vibrations to 'ether waves' and 'the subconscious'. One of the favourites, however, has always been magnetism. Many people have been convinced that Man has a separate sense devoted to geographical direction based on a direct awareness of the Earth's magnetism (Viguier 1882, Hudson 1922, Lucannas 1924, reviewed by Jaccard 1931). The popular belief is that it exists primarily in 'primitive' people and children. Serious attempts to obtain evidence, however, have been few. Warren (1908) described a boy with what he called a magnetic sense of direction, though Warren was unsuccessful in his attempts to disorient the boy. Twenty-two years later, this person was located (De Silva 1931) but disclaimed ever having had a magnetic sense. De Silva described another boy, twelve years old, who had such a well-developed sense of direction that he could orient correctly in any compass direction. There was no evidence, however, that this ability was based on reference to the Earth's magnetic field, and the most recent review of the effects of the geomagnetic field on Man could find no evidence for a geomagnetic sense of direction (Ketchen, Porter and Bolton 1978).

Aside from non-industrialist peoples and children, most attention in relation to the sixth sense has been directed toward the blind. The facility shown by blind people to detect the direction and distance of obstacles in their path puzzled scientists at least as far back as 1749 (Gatty 1958). In that year, Diderot concluded that a blind acquaintance judged the proximity of obstacles by increased sensitivity of his facial nerves, using his cheeks as 'feelers'. The truth of the matter for blind people was not finally demonstrated until Supa et al. (1944) took the step of blocking the ears of blind subjects who then invariably bumped into obstacles in their path. The answer did not lie in the realms of magnetism but in a primitive form of echolocation, a suggestion first made in the first decade of the twentieth century by Heller and Truschel (see Gatty 1958). As a man approaches an obstacle, the sounds of his footsteps rise steadily in pitch. Nowadays, sophisticated mechanical aids to echolocation have been developed to enable blind people to move around without striking obstacles.

By the beginning of the 1970s, therefore, few scientists took seriously any claim that humans, or any other animal for that matter, had a sense of direction involving reference to the Earth's magnetic field. The disclaimers voiced their feelings powerfully, whether for birds (e.g. Matthews 1968) or for humans. Gatty (1958) proclaimed strongly his disbelief in the sixth sense and asserted that a Man with a good sense of direction is simply an able pathfinder; somebody who can find his way 'by use of the five senses' and a knowledge of 'how to interpret nature's signs'. Howard and Templeton (1966) stress that no good experimental evidence has ever been produced in support of the hypothesis of a magnetic sense of direction and Lewis (1972) considered a 'notable feature' of his studies of Polynesian navigation that not once did anyone lay claim to a sixth sense of any sort. Finally, as recently as 1979, in discussing the tremendous strides being made in the study of the magnetic sense of direction in other organisms, Stephen Jay Gould was able to comment: 'What an imperceptible lot we are . . . The paranormal may be a fantasy . . . but parahuman powers of (magnetic) perception lie all about us in birds, bees and bacteria' (Gould 1979).

Contemporary opinion, therefore, is unlikely to approve of any suggestion that the new-found ability of humans for route-based navigation derives, when blindfold, from a magnetic sense of direction. Indeed, the grounds for extending the study of such navigation to look for a magnetic sense might have seemed fairly weak had it not been for the simultaneous developments in the study of Homing Pigeons and other organisms (reviewed in Schmidt-Koenig and Keeton 1978, Ketchen et al. 1978, Schmidt-Koenig 1979, Baker 1978, 1980).

Some mud-dwelling bacteria always swim toward the north side of a petri dish, but can be made to change direction by changing the magnetic field with a Helmholtz coil. Among invertebrates, many have now been found to take directional cues from the Earth's magnetic field, including planarians, mud snails, and Honey Bees, **Apis mellifera**. Amongst fish, elasmobranchs at least have been shown to have a magnetic sense of direction. Kalmijn has shown that individuals trained to rest on one side of a circular tank can be induced to rest on some other side by experimental alteration of the magnetic field. Salamanders have also been shown to have a magnetic sense of direction but so far little attention has been paid to reptiles. However, bar magnets attached to the shell of Green Turtles, **Chelonia mydas**, seemed to disrupt their ability to orient toward home after experimental displacement from a nesting beach. Finally, several species of birds, among them Ring-billed Gulls, **Larus delawarensis**, and Eurasian Robins, **Erithacus rubecula** (Fig. 6.1), as well as Homing Pigeons, have now been shown to have a magnetic sense of direction. At the rate a magnetic sense of direction is being discovered in different animals, it seems (Baker 1980) that the final search may be for an animal that does not have such a sense. The only major group that, so far, has not been demonstrated to have a magnetic sense of direction is mammals.

This is not to say that magnetic fields have no influence on mammals, only that they have not yet been demonstrated to provide directional cues. The brain impulses of rabbits are influenced by changes in the magnetic field as also is their reaction to light and sound. High field strength over a long period affects the spleen, bone marrow, and liver of mice. Influences have also been recorded on the longevity, vigour, aggression, ageing, appetite, and conception rate of mice and rats. Monkeys show an effect on heart rate and function (Ketchen et al. 1978).

In view of the danger of clinical effects, few direct physiological experiments have been carried out on humans. Reported symptoms of high field strengths (1·5–2T) have been a taste sensation in the mouth and a slight sensation of pain in filled teeth. Soviet workers engaged in fabrication of permanent

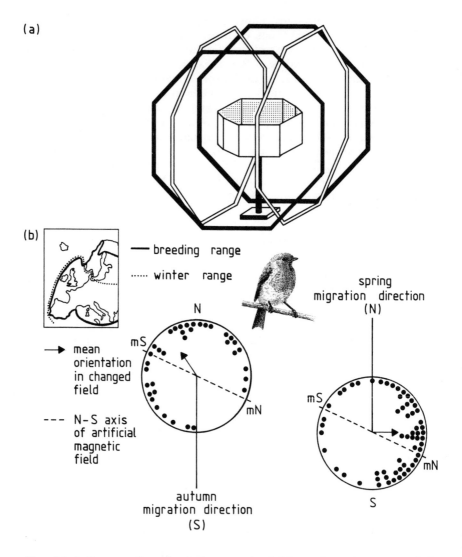

Fig. 6.1 Influence of a changed magnetic field on the orientation of the European Robin, Erithacus rubecula, *a seasonal migrant*

(a) Orientation cage and Helmholtz coil system used by Wiltschko

(b) Influence of a changed magnetic field on orientation in spring and summer Each dot is the mean angle for an individual as calculated from one night's exposure in an orientation cage. Vertical line shows the traditional migration direction at each time of year. mN, mS show magnetic north and magnetic south of the changed magnetic field. Other evidence presented by Wiltschko suggests that it is the angle magnetic lines of force make to the horizontal that is important, rather than their polarity.

(Re-drawn from Schmidt-Koenig (1979) and Baker (1978) after Wiltschko)

magnets have reported such symptoms as irritability, fatigue, occasional dizziness, altered appetite, headache, changes in heart function, decrease in arterial blood pressure, itching, burning, numbness and marbling pattern in hands, as well as changes in brain impulses. Various clinicians have sought correlations between magnetic storms and the incidence of nervous disorders, suicides, admissions to mental hospitals, and admissions of heart-failure patients to intensive-care units. Often, though not always, positive relationships have been found (Ketchen *et al.* 1978). Finally, there has been recent speculation, and a little serious evidence, that minute muscular contractions may be influenced by local anomalies in the Earth's magnetic field and that this may be the basis of dowsing, the art of discovering water or metals under ground (Williamson 1979).

All of this implies that human physiology is sensitive to magnetic fields but does nothing to suggest a magnetic sense of direction. Moreover, before the Barnard Castle experiment, the only serious attempt in recent years to investigate such a sense of direction produced negative results. Beischer (1971), as part of study into the biological effects on astronauts of changed or reduced magnetic fields, exposed men to a reduced, virtually null, magnetic field within a large Helmholtz-coil system. Pairs of men were exposed for up to 2 weeks to fields below 50×10^{-9} T. A variety of standard physiological and psychological tests were carried out but no influence of the reduced field could be detected. Among the spatial orientation tasks carried out were:

1. having to adjust rows of lights to apparent parallelism;
2. indicating by pointing the position that a point of light had last been seen on a screen;
3. estimating the distance from the midline of the forehead that was touched by the experimenter with the point of a pencil;
4. copying sample drawings.

No effects were found. Standard tests for visual fields and acuity were carried out as were tests for estimating time. Again, no effects were found. Finally, the subjects' equilibrium was tested by standing or walking on a narrow rail. Again, no effects were found. None of these tasks, however, is an appropriate test of the ability with which a magnetic sense of direction now seems most likely to be involved: route-based navigation over distances of kilometres. This was the situation that the Barnard Castle experiment was the first to attempt to study.

Thirty-one subjects took part in the second of the two Barnard Castle experiments. Of these, 15 placed at the back of their head a bar-magnet held in position by the elastic of their blindfold. The remaining 16 controls placed a brass bar of dimensions similar to the real magnets ($7.5 \times 1.5 \times 0.5$ cm) in the same position. All of the subjects thought they were wearing a real magnet. Seating was arranged in blocks within the coach with the intent that subjects without magnets would be beyond the field of influence of the real magnets worn by others. However, some interaction must have occurred. Other details of this, the last experiment in Series II, are as described in Chapter 3.

The results of the Barnard Castle experiment are shown in Fig. 6.2. At the first stop, about 5 km SW of home, the experimentals' estimate of home

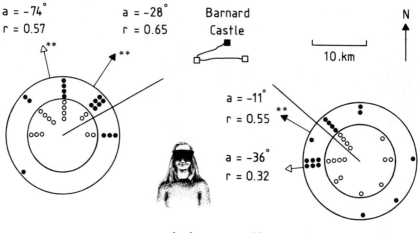

●▲ controls   ○△ with magnets

Fig. 6.2 The second Barnard Castle experiment: influence of bar magnets on the route-based navigation of humans

Each dot is one individual's written estimate of home direction while still blindfold. Controls wore brass bars tucked in the elastic of their blindfold at the back of the head. Experimentals wore bar magnets in the same way (see also Fig. 10.5).

direction is significantly in error by $74°$ in an anticlockwise direction. The controls' estimate of home direction is not significantly in error but is also shifted anticlockwise, this time by $28°$. The two mean angles are significantly different at the 10% level ($F_{1,29} = 3.57$) but not quite at the 5% level ($F_{crit} = 4.18$). The subjects were given no indication of their actual position at the first stop and the coach moved on to a second position, about 5 km SE of home. This time only the controls produced an estimate of home direction that was significantly non-uniform.

These results were sufficiently surprising and encouraging for Series III experiments to be designed specifically to test for a magnetic sense of direction. The broad details of Series III have been described in Chapter 3. So far unmentioned, however, is that throughout the Series III experiments, all subjects wore PVC helmets (Fig. 6.3) designed at Manchester by Dr Stuart Bailey. These helmets supported two lateral coils, each of 200 turns of 40 s.w.g. copper, covering the braincase. A 50 mA current from a 9 V battery passed through both coils produced a magnetic field at the centre of the helmet 3.5 times the horizontal component of the Earth's field.

The experiment was designed on the assumption that the same 32 subjects would be available during the four journeys that made up Series III. Each helmet was identified by a number positioned so that it could not be seen by the experimenters while the helmet was being worn. Subjects wore the same helmet on each of the journeys.

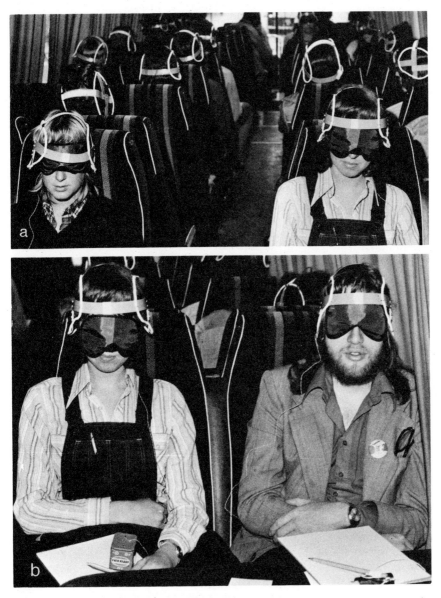

Fig. 6.3 Helmets used in the Manchester (Series III) experiments on the influence of a changed magnetic field on route-based navigation

(a) Lateral Helmholtz coils are supported by PVC helmets and connected to a 9 V battery. The direction or absence of flow of the current depended on connections, or their absence, in the small white box on the back of the helmet (b) On the first journey of Series III, 6 subjects had to sit with their backs to the direction of travel. On the remaining three journeys, all subjects faced forwards.

(Photos by Les Lockey)

Over the four journeys, each helmet was connected with north once to the right and once to the left of the skull (R- and L-helmets), and twice was disconnected (controls). This meant that each subject was a control twice and an R-helmet and L-helmet experimental once each. The subjects were encouraged to believe that all their helmets were magnetically active and were given no details until the series was complete. Each subject sat once in the front right, front left, rear right, and rear left quarters of the coach and on each journey two R-helmets, two L-helmets, and four controls sat in each quarter. They were asked to face directly forwards as much as comfort allowed and were also asked not to talk.

In practice, the same 32 subjects were not always available. On all but the first occasion there were absentees and two stand-ins, 1 male, 1 female, were employed to fill any gaps. Moreover, routine checks after each journey revealed that on two occasions, a single helmet had been connected incorrectly, influencing the distribution of controls and R- and L-helmets. The composition of experimentals and controls on each journey with regard to sex is summarised in Table 6.1.

Table 6.1 Numbers of male and female experimentals and controls during the four journeys of Series III

Week	Controls		R-helmets		Experimentals L-helmets		Total		Total	
	♂	♀	♂	♀	♂	♀	♂	♀	♂	♀
1	10	6	4	4	4	4	8	8	18	14
2	8	5	5	4	5	3	10	7	18	12
3	8	8	5	3	5	3	10	6	18	14
4	10	6	4	3	3	5	7	8	17	14
Total	36	25	18	14	17	15	35	29	71	54

The changed magnetic field of the experimentals had no effect on their estimation of distance (Fig. 6.4) but had a marked influence on the estimation of direction. Figure 6.5 summarises the written estimates obtained while still blindfold at the final position on each of the four journeys. A clear, but complex, influence of the magnets can be seen. Mean angle for the controls is always within $30°$ of the true direction and at three of the four locations the distributions are significantly non-uniform. For all the experimentals combined, the distributions are significantly non-uniform only on day 3. Moreover, on day 2, R- and L-helmet estimates have mean angles that are significantly different. There seems no doubt that the altered magnetic field is influencing the ability for route-based navigation, but that the extent and nature of this influence depends either on the direction of travel or on the complexity of the outward journey. We can gain some insight into this influence by analysing the reconstructions of the outward tracks described in Chapter 3.

Figure 6.6 compares the angles between successive legs of the outward journeys as estimated by experimentals and controls. There is a clear effect of

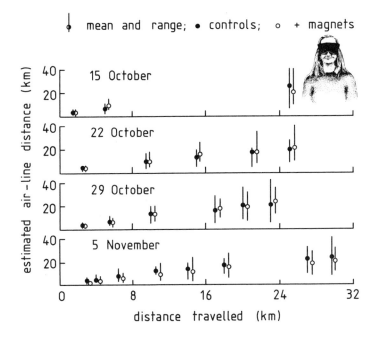

Fig. 6.4 *Lack of influence of changed magnetic field on estimate of distance from home*

the altered magnetic field. R-helmet wearers can distinguish anticlockwise turns from clockwise, but seem unable to judge the extent of anticlockwise turns, assessing them all to be about 60°. L-helmet wearers seem as able as controls to judge anticlockwise turns but, when turning clockwise by 90° or less, judge that they are still turning anticlockwise. When all data are lumped relative to actual angle of turn, R- and L-helmet mean angles are significantly different as are the mean angles for L-helmets and controls.

There are two ways that an estimate of mean angle between legs can be obtained. One is by monitoring the angles of turn of the coach. The other is by estimating the direction of each leg of the journey relatively independently of the direction of the previous leg. The first method depends on a correct orientation during the initial memorised-map phase of the journey. Thereafter, as long as all errors in estimating angles cancel out, the final estimate of direction will be reasonably accurate. Once lost, however, a sense of location cannot be regained (Fig. 5.9). The method that involves judgement of the direction of each leg is not so dependent on initial accuracy during the memorised-map phase. Moreover, even once a sense of location has been lost, it can be regained, at least approximately (Fig. 5.9).

Figure 6.7 analyses the reconstructed tracks with respect to the estimated direction of each leg. This ability seems much more pronounced than any ability to measure angle between legs, but is strongly influenced both by the

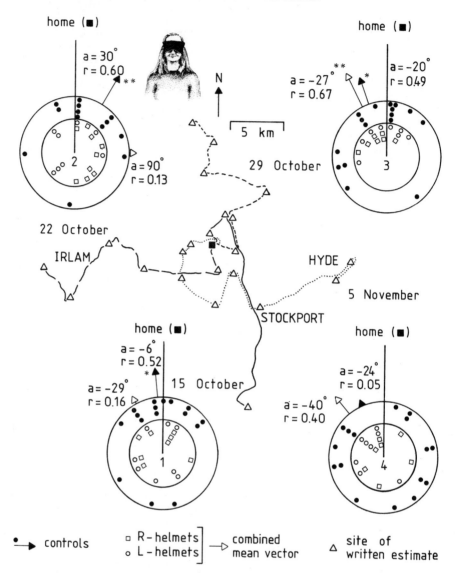

Fig. 6.5 *Influence of changed magnetic field on final written estimate (while still blindfold) of home direction*

altered magnetic fields and by the direction of travel. For the lumped data presented, the mean vectors for controls are all within 24° of the actual direction of travel and are significantly non-uniform. Only when travelling

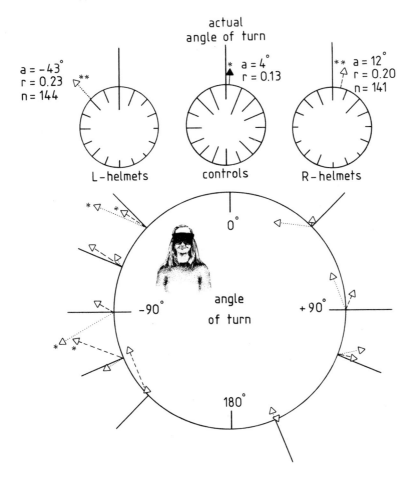

Fig. 6.6 *Influence of changed magnetic field during displacement on the estimate of angle of turn between successive legs*

Calculated from reconstructed outward journeys (Fig. 3.11). Conventions as in Fig. 5.11.

between west and north are the data for combined experimentals significantly non-uniform. When travelling between north and east the mean angle for the combined experimentals is significantly anti-clockwise of that for controls. Between east and west (through south) mean angles for R- and L-helmets are significantly different, the R-helmet estimates also being significantly different from the controls. Between west and north there is no significant difference between the estimates of the experimentals and the controls.

Further evidence that it is the direction of each leg that is being estimated, rather than the angle between legs, is given in Fig. 6.8. This analyses in more detail the effect shown in the previous chapter of the recovery of the sense of

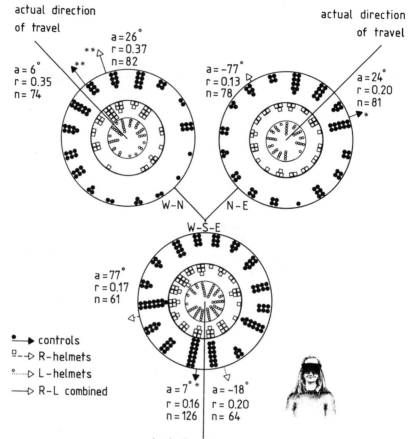

Fig. 6.7 Influence of changed magnetic field during displacement on the estimation of direction of travel during each leg

Each dot is one individual's estimate of direction of travel during one leg of displacement, as calculated from the reconstructed outward journeys. As the estimate for each leg should be relatively independent of the preceding estimate, data can justifiably be lumped. Leg directions are lumped according to three categories as shown.

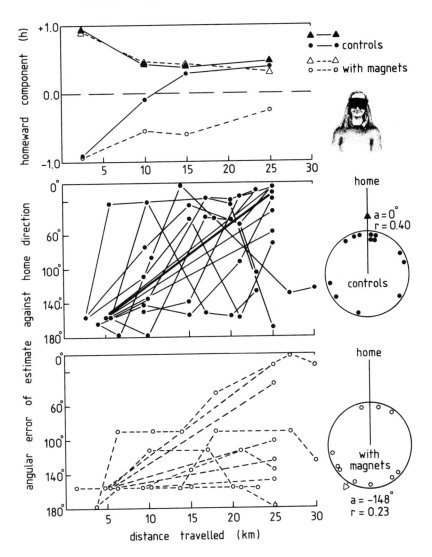

Fig. 6.8 *Influence of a changed magnetic field during displacement on the recovery of individuals disoriented during the initial 5 km of the journey*

Conventions as in Fig. 5.10. Lower two graphs show the sequence for individuals. All controls recover to within 60° of the home direction, even if subsequently they become disoriented once more. Only 30 per cent of those wearing magnets recover even to within 90° of the home direction. Controls and experimentals 180° ± 30° in error within the first 5 km produce mean angles at the final position as shown that are significantly different ($F_{1,21} = 5.574; P < 0.05$).

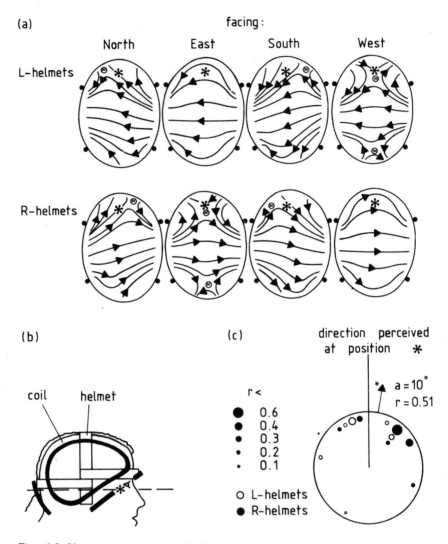

Fig. 6.9 *Variation in magnetic fields induced by Helmholtz coils in relation to direction of travel and the predicted position of the human magnetic sense organ*

(a) Variation in horizontal component of magnetic field at different positions in the head in relation to direction of travel. Arrow heads point in same direction as north-seeking arm of magnetic compass. ⊗, null point at which lines of force run vertically. Only the horizontal component of the field is shown. At no position, however, is the vertical component reversed relative to the horizontal component, though inevitably the angle of inclination varies considerably.

(b) Side view of head to show the plane at which (a) is drawn and the predicted position of the magnetic sense organ (✳)

(c) Comparison of observed and expected estimates of direction of travel if the

location of individuals that are effectively lost by the end of the map-following phase. This recovery is consistent with an estimation of direction and emphasises the way that the altered magnetic field hinders the recovery. All of the 'lost' controls regain their sense of location, even if subsequently they lose it once more. On the other hand, 70 per cent of those with activated helmets fail to recover to within 90° of the true direction.

The Series III experiments thus have begun to unravel the mechanism of route-based navigation by blindfolded humans, which we may now summarise as follows. Over the first two or so kilometres, memorised-map following is used but soon gives way to an alternative system based on estimation of the direction of travel. The main sense used is an unconscious magnetic sense of direction, perhaps backed up when possible by detection of the direction of heat from the sun. Continuous assessment of direction from home may be reassessed in the light of any olfactory or acoustic landmarks that may be detected, but rarely, it seems, are these given more weight than the continuous assessment. For example, subjects wearing activated helmets also heard the planes coming in to land at Manchester airport on day 1 but rejected this information in favour of their continuous assessment. Only controls that already thought they were south of Manchester made use of the information to confirm their assessment. Although subjects make a conscious attempt to detect angles of turn, the ability to do so is weak and certainly secondary to judgement of direction.

Activated helmets, producing an altered magnetic field through the head, have a number of significant effects. First, they influence the estimation of direction. Secondly, they influence the ability to judge angles of turn, having the tendency to make people more consistent but wider of the mark. Thirdly, however, and perhaps most significantly, they prevent subjects, once lost, from recovering their sense of direction. The result is that magnet wearers show a steady deterioration in accuracy over the course of the journey.

When the experiments for Series III were designed, it was naïvely assumed that the helmets would induce a fixed magnetic field through the subject's head. The result should have been an inability to detect changes in angle relative to the magnetic field and consequent assessment that the direction of travel was unchanging. Thus, subjects wearing R-helmets, with north to the right of the head, might have been expected always to consider they were travelling west, while those wearing L-helmets should always consider they

---

sense organ were located at the position shown in (b) ●, *R-helmet estimates;* ○, *L-helmet estimates (as from Fig. 6.7 but for 6 different directions, not 4). Although both angle and length of the mean vectors for these estimates are indicated, only the mean angles are used in the second-order analysis presented. Vertical line, expected estimate of direction; arrow, calculated second-order mean vector. Any point on the thick oblique lines at the front and back of the head in (b) would give the same match between expected and observed estimates. No other positions in the head give a significant match. The asterisk marks the only position that is not within the nasal cavity or bone, etc. It is more or less in the region beneath the olfactory bulb of the brain.*

(Modified from Baker and Bailey MS)

were travelling east. The results (Fig. 6.7) do not support such a simple model and the fact that assessment of direction by experimentals is influenced by direction of travel suggests that the artificial magnetic field is interacting with, rather than overriding, the Earth's magnetic field.

Figure 6.9 shows a plot of the horizontal component of the magnetic field inside the helmets at a single plane through the head and for different compass orientations. It can be seen that, whereas the magnetic field varies little in the centre of the head, at the periphery there is marked interaction with the Earth's magnetic field. This suggests that the sense organ that is the basis of the magnetic sense of direction is located peripherally rather than centrally. We can go further. Taking different positions in the head, predictions can be made for the perceived direction if each position was the location of the sense organ. These predictions can then be compared with the observed influence of the helmets on estimated direction of travel. Only at one realistic position is there a strong similarity between the two (Fig. 6.9). This is a point at the front of the head, between but slightly below the eyes in the mid-line and approximately 3 cm in from the front edge of the helmet. Interestingly, a similar midline position would fit with the 74° deflection when travelling SW observed during the first leg of the Barnard Castle experiment. These similarities suggest that the magnetic sense organ in humans is situated more or less in the region beneath the olfactory bulb of the brain.

When the reality of a magnetic sense was finally accepted for pigeons, in the mid-1970s, the search began in earnest for the sense organ that was involved. Walcott and Green (1974) had managed to change pigeon orientation during homing experiments by the use of a cap-and-collar Helmholtz coil system (Fig. 6.10). This at least suggested that the sense organ was in the bird's head. Leask (1977) suggested that magnetic fields may be perceived, as long as there is some light, as a by-product of the normal visual process through rhodopsin or similar molecules. The energy required would be provided by optical pumping. At the time of writing, however, the chief contender for the magnetic sense organ is a small (2 × 1 mm) deposit of magnetite particles located between the dura mater of the brain and the skull (Walcott et al. 1979). Often the organ is so close against the skull that it is difficult to separate. The organ is supplied by nerves and blood vessels and appears to be unpaired. Its precise position, however, is as yet undescribed.

Magnetite particles also appear to be the basis of the magnetic sense in both bacteria and Honey Bees. In all three cases they are assumed, and have the correct dimensions (Frankel et al. 1979), to function as small compass needles, aligning themselves to the Earth's magnetic field whenever the organism changes direction, thus stimulating the cell(s) containing them and providing directional information. The next step is to examine the human head to see if it also has a magnetic-based sense organ in the position indicated by the Manchester experiments.

As in any scientific field, there is now an urgent need for the Series III experiments to be replicated by other workers in other places. The results from the combined Barnard Castle and Manchester experiments, however, are so

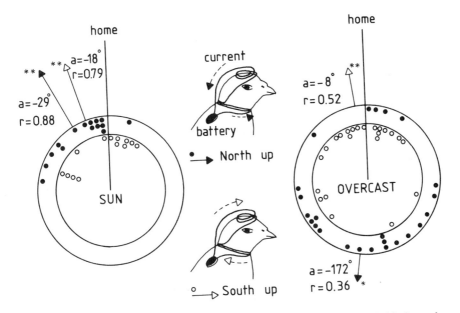

Fig. 6.10 *Influence of reversed vertical component of magnetic field through head on the initial orientation of pigeons*

When released under sun, changed magnetic fields have little, if any, effect. Under overcast, birds released for the first time are strongly influenced. (Modified from Schmidt-Koenig (1979) after Walcott and Green)

strong that it will be surprising if they cannot be repeated elsewhere. Even if the results are confirmed by other workers, it is a fairly safe prediction that many people will still be reluctant to accept the conclusion that Man, like so many other animals, has a magnetic sense of direction. The reason for such reluctance is obvious: we are not conscious of such a sense, and many people find it difficult to accept that they have senses of which they are not directly aware. This is clearly unreasonable, but the point has to be answered. Why is the magnetic sense unconscious? Why is it that not even the natural navigators of the world, such as the Polynesians, lay claim to such a sense? What is the role of such a sense in real navigation, as opposed to its role in an experimental situation?

All of these are important questions and demand answers if we are to believe that Man does have a magnetic sense of direction and that this sense does fill an important role in natural navigation. Such questions are discussed in Chapter 10 in the perspective of the next two chapters which deal respectively with location-based navigation and navigation in action among the world's natural navigators.

7

Location-based navigation: mental maps and a sense of place

Location-based navigation is the ability to recognise location from an examination of the immediate environment and from this recognition to work out the direction of home. Theoretically, two main mechanisms are available to any animal. One is to make use of familiar landmarks, relate these to some mental map, and from this map to work out required directions. The other is to make use of larger-scale features, such as the sun, moon, stars or magnetic field, and to calculate direction from the geographical coordinates thus derived. The first mechanism makes use of a familiar-area map, the second makes use of a grid map.

In order to study location-based navigation, it is necessary to be able to divorce it from route-based navigation. This has rarely been possible for non-human animals. Schmidt-Koenig (1979) has reviewed the evidence for Homing Pigeons and concluded that they use location-based navigation both at the release site and *en route* home after release. Analysis has shown that the last five pigeons to be released home significantly faster than the first five out of a sample of 20 released within 2–3 h. This could indicate that information may be perceived or processed by the birds while sitting in their canvas-covered crates at the release site. Keeton has also found an inverse correlation between time of release and vanishing time, again supporting this view. Finally, birds that do not depart precisely toward home nevertheless home successfully, suggesting that corrections of initially false directions must take place *en route*. This is further supported by the absence, reported by Keeton, of a correlation between vanishing bearings and homing speeds. The most direct evidence, however, comes from radio-tracking birds or following them by helicopter or light plane during their homing flight. Birds that initially set off in the wrong direction eventually correct their orientation toward home, though often not until they have flown tens of kilometres.

The cues used by birds in location-based navigation are poorly known, though evidently visual landmarks play some part. Herring Gulls, **Larus argentatus**, displaced from breeding colonies on the shores of Lake Huron, when released on the shore of another lake, spend their time flying along the shore-line until their urge to home wanes (Southern 1971). Wagner (1972) has shown that large-scale topographical features, such as mountains and lakes, influence the vanishing points of Homing Pigeons. The most ingenious study, however, has been that by Köhler (1978) who developed a simple camera to be attached onto the bird's head. Through an aperture on top of the camera the sun forms a spot on the horizontal film each time the bird holds its head steady

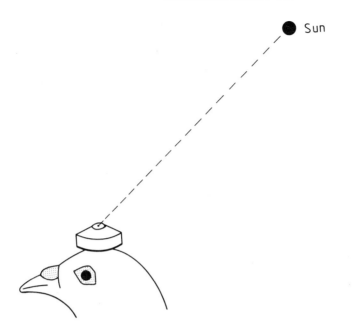

Fig. 7.1 Simple camera attached to pigeon's head used by Köhler to record the direction in which a pigeon fixes its attention during initial orientation

A shutter closed the aperture after 60 s.
(Re-drawn from Schmidt-Koenig (1979) after Köhler)

for a few seconds. With the position of the sun known to the experimenter, the direction of fixation whenever the head is held steady can be determined. Köhler suggests that after release the pigeons systematically scan the horizon and take special note of horizon features. Scanning is more intense when visibility is only 12 km than when it is 30 km.

Caged Starlings, **Sturnus vulgaris**, taught to discriminate between locations 200 km apart, could only continue to do so as long as both the sun and distant landmarks were visible (Cavé *et al.* 1974). Experiments by Kramer and Wallraff (in Baker 1978, Schmidt-Koenig 1979) on Homing Pigeons confined in aviaries from birth led to a similar conclusion. As long as the birds could see the sun and all 360° of the distant horizon while confined in the aviary, there was evidence that the ability to navigate, at least from 150 km to the south of the home loft, could be developed (Fig. 7.2). This theme of the importance to navigation of distant visual landmarks and a compass, such as the sun, is a recurring one and is found again when we consider humans.

When available, therefore, vision may be used in location-based navigation, particularly with regard to horizon features. In a series of experiments in which Homing Pigeons have been released wearing frosted-glass lenses, Schmidt-Koenig (1979) has been able to show that visual impairment does not reduce homeward orientation. These data have not yet been shown, however, to be relevant to location-based navigation. Apart from the fact that there

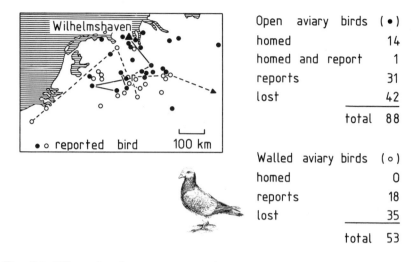

Open aviary birds (•)	
homed	14
homed and report	1
reports	31
lost	42
total	88

Walled aviary birds (○)	
homed	0
reports	18
lost	35
total	53

Fig. 7.2 Effect of early experience on homing performance of pigeons

Pigeons were raised in aviaries near Wilhelmshaven and not allowed out before displacement/release to site r. Pigeons raised in open aviaries showed some homing ability. Pigeons raised in aviaries with opaque walls so that they could see the sky but not the horizon showed no indication of being able to determine home direction from r.

(Re-drawn from Baker (1978) after Kramer)

must be some doubt whether the birds were unable to detect horizon features (Baker 1978), the birds could be orientating toward home solely on the basis of route-based navigation. Demonstration that these frosted-lens birds were adopting their orientation in relation to a sun compass (Schmidt-Koenig and Keeton 1977) supports this possibility. If by route-based navigation the birds have determined they are, say, north of home, they need only a compass at the release site in order to set off for the south.

Although the frosted-lens experiments themselves may tell us little, if anything, about location-based navigation, there is no doubt that non-visual cues can be used by pigeons. The neatest demonstration is that by Papi and his co-workers (Papi *et al.* 1974). Two groups of pigeons were raised in aviaries walled with plastic and bamboo so that air could enter diffusely. In addition the birds had access to the two glass-walled corridors on top of the aviary through which air repeatedly was blown. One group had the volatile components of olive oil added when the air was blown from the south and synthetic turpentine from the north. The other group received the same treatment in reverse. At the release point, a drop of olive oil was applied to the beak of half the experimental birds and turpentine to the other half. In releases from the east of the loft, birds with olive oil on their beaks flew to the north if they had received olive oil at the loft with south winds and to the south if they had received it with north winds. The same effect was found with the turpentine birds. Although homing speed was not affected, suggesting the birds rapidly switched to other cues, the results suggest strongly that birds do take note of olfactory landmarks.

Studies of animals other than birds have produced few data on location-based navigation. Cricket Frogs, **Acris gryllus**, caged on an unfamiliar shore showed evidence of having learned to orient to their new surroundings within 2 h, and the process is nearly complete within 24–48 h, but only if the frogs are allowed to see the daytime sky. Once allowed to see this sky, the frogs could orient to the new shore in both day and night tests. Yet again there is an implication that landmarks and compass information are used for location-based navigation. Sounds are also memorised in relation to the compass direction from which they are heard. Chorus Frogs, **Pseudacris triseriata**, caged for several days near a breeding chorus of their own species, then displaced and released in an arena, selected a compass direction that would have taken them to the chorus from the original site but not from the site of testing (Ferguson 1971).

Wood Mice, **Apodemus sylvaticus**, orient in the home direction more consistently at release distances of up to 80 m when they can see the surrounding vegetation than when they can only see the sky (Mather and Baker 1980). This suggests they have a mental map of visual familiar landmarks that can be used in location-based navigation. Indeed, most research into the mental maps of non-humans has involved a rodent, the laboratory rat, though other than demonstrating that such a map exists, little progress has been made (Olton 1977). Chimpanzees, **Pan troglodytes**, show some ability to read maps (Menzel *et al.* 1978).

The ability to read and draw maps has received major attention from psychologists in their study of the mental maps of humans (Howard and Templeton 1966, Gould and White 1974, Canter 1977). Kaplan (1973) has argued that an innate ability to build up mental maps is an evolutionary necessity to Man, without which hunting would have been impossible. While not disputing this, it seems likely that all animals that live within a familiar area (i.e. probably all vertebrates and a variety of invertebrates) have equal need for a mental map, and it has been argued (Baker 1981a) that all have a sense of location comparable in every way with that possessed by humans.

The study of human mental maps has shown that everybody normally has a more or less adequate imaginary map. Although these are frequently distorted with respect to distance and directions, they are nevertheless functional. Only subjects with damage to particular areas of the brain have grossly distorted maps that prevent them from finding their way around (Fig. 7.3) (Critchley 1953). The part of the brain most involved in mental-map making is not known with certainty though a recent case has been made out for it being the hippocampus (O'Keefe and Nadel 1979).

A functional map is a prime requirement for location-based navigation. The information stored can often be fairly subtle, yet still useful. For example, many people, when shown a photograph, are often able to guess where it was taken, mainly from the natural topography but also from more detailed cues such as plants, animals, soil and rock formations, buildings and, of course, the people (Gatty 1958). When such a location can be placed on the mental map, the direction of home can be estimated. During the Manchester experiments, subjects occasionally resorted, once the blindfolds had been removed, to

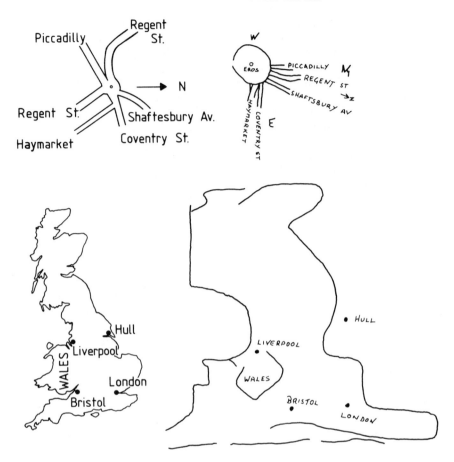

Fig. 7.3 *Distorted maps drawn by a human patient with a right parietal lesion*
Note the neglect of left-hand landmarks in the plan of Piccadilly Circus, London,
(top) and the shift of topographical detail toward the right in the map of England
and Wales (bottom).
(Compiled from Critchley 1953)

saying that the area 'felt' like North Manchester or Cheshire, etc., and then took their bearings from the sun accordingly.

Before the visual estimates can be considered, however, there is one other factor that must be taken into account. In the experiments of Series III, when displacement was by coach, a number of subjects complained that they lost their bearings at the last minute while being led blindfold out of the coach. Figure 7.4 checks and supports this claim by comparing the results for Series I and III.

The ability to point in the home direction while still blindfold in Series I was influenced by conditions at the release site, being better on days when the sun was shining and/or the wind blowing (Fig. 7.5). Subjects claimed to have

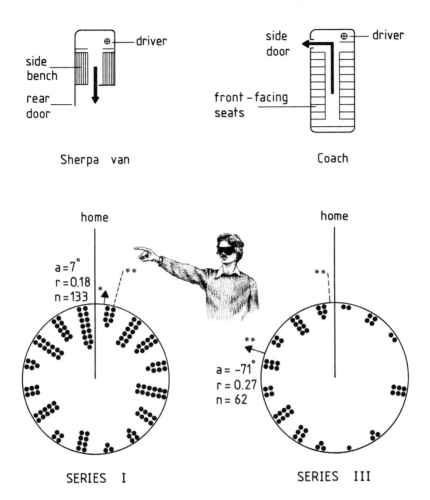

Fig. 7.4 *Apparent influence of vehicle on translation of written or verbal estimates of home direction into a proposed direction for travel*

Each dot is one individual's estimate of home direction as indicated after disboarding by pointing while still blindfolded. Mean vector for the estimate by pointing (solid arrow) is compared with the mean vector for the last (verbal or written) estimate made before disboarding (dashed vector). Vehicles used are shown in plan view. Solid arrow shows path taken while disboarding.

judged the direction of sun and wind from the feeling of heat or air on the face. Evidently, subjects were taking their estimate of the compass direction of home as derived from route-based navigation and attempting to translate this into an actual direction by referring to some external compass cue. Many of the subjects had noted wind direction during their visit to the University roof before the experiment began.

On journey 1 of Series III, the subjects removed their helmets before getting

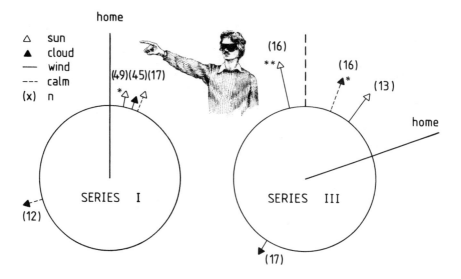

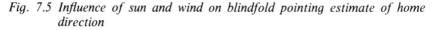

Fig. 7.5 Influence of sun and wind on blindfold pointing estimate of home direction

In the Series III diagram, the figure has been rotated by the 71° bias suggested in Fig. 7.4 to be due to disorientation caused by disboarding the coach. More data are needed. The sun seems implicated, but if this were being used to translate the final written estimate into a pointed direction, there should not have been the 71° rotation observed during Series III.

off the coach and pointing. On journeys 2–4, the helmets remained on and activated. The influence of the magnets is still apparent in the blindfold pointing (Fig. 7.7) but disappears when the blindfolds and helmets are removed. So too does the 90° anticlockwise shift that was evident in Fig. 7.4. These two changes indicate that visual location-based navigation is taking place.

The ability to point in the homeward direction once the blindfolds come off is also influenced by conditions at the release site and by the clues that the subjects opt to use. Figure 7.8 compares visual estimates according to the cues that the subjects claimed to have used. It can be seen that the best estimates are made by those subjects that claimed to have used a reliable compass (i.e. sun and/or wind) and/or distant horizon landmarks. Some subjects, on days that the sun's disc was not visible, but the cloud was broken, claimed to have used the area of brightest sky to indicate the sun's direction. Such estimates are relatively inaccurate. Yet other subjects used near-distance landmarks, such as buildings, as a cue. In particular, any group of near-distance buildings was often interpreted as indicating the direction of the Manchester conurbation. Such estimates were also unreliable. So, too, were those described by the subjects as pure guesses. The most potent cause of error, however, was found

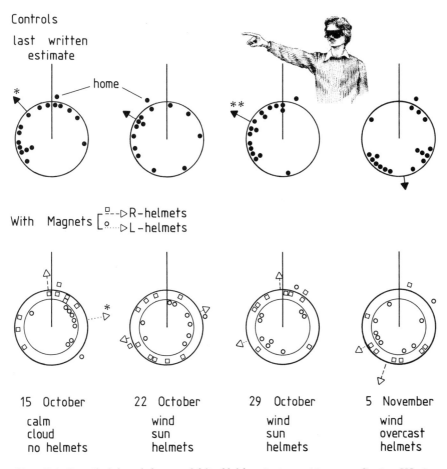

Fig. 7.6 *Detailed breakdown of blindfold pointing estimates, Series III, in relation to prevailing conditions*

Vertical line shows the mean direction for the last written estimate while on the coach. Diagram reflects, therefore, the accuracy of translating the written estimate into a pointed direction. True home direction is shown by the symbol outside the circle. Interpretation is confused by the 71° rotation demonstrated in Fig. 7.4 and by the apparent 180° error of both controls and experimentals on 5 November (perhaps related to the 180° turn made by the coach between penultimate and final positions (Fig. 6.5)). There is a hint that the translation of the written estimate while pointing is influenced by the changed magnetic field, but this part of the experiment needs re-designing before the influence can properly be determined.

for subjects that thought they recognised the release site as one they had visited before but were in fact mistaken.

A demonstration that use of a reliable compass produces an accurate

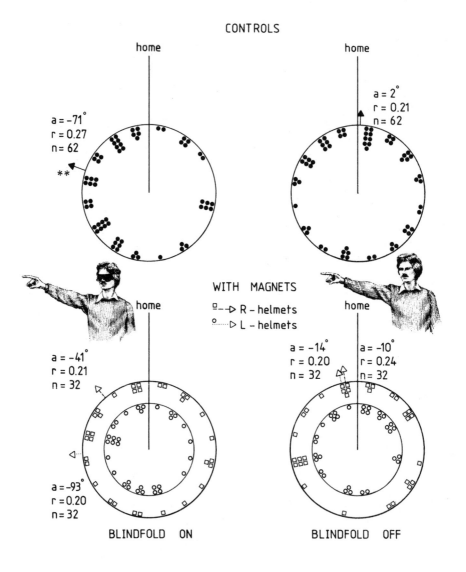

Fig. 7.7 When blindfolds are removed the influence of the changed magnetic field during the outward journey and the rotation due to disboarding the coach disappear, thus indicating the occurrence of visual, location-based navigation.

estimate of home direction proves little in relation to location-based navigation. It could indicate simply that the subject is using a compass to translate the route-based estimate into a visual estimate (as suggested for

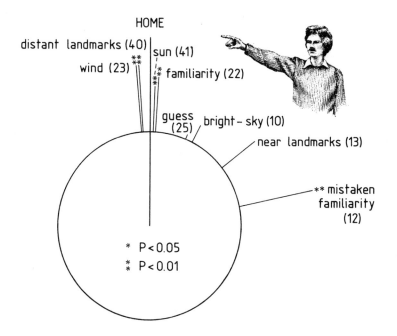

Fig. 7.8 Influence of cues used on estimate of home direction when blindfolds are removed (Series I)

Numbers in brackets are of sample size. Lines are mean vectors

pigeons with frosted-glass lenses). In order to control for this possibility it is necessary to examine whether use of a compass is involved in an actual improvement of the visual estimate over the route-based estimate. This can be done simply by noting how many individuals produce a better estimate of home direction when sighted than when blindfolded. Table 7.1 shows which factors lead to an improvement in the visual estimate over the route-based estimates (written or verbal). In fact, because the route-based estimates are so good, there is little room for improvement and most cues are associated with a deterioration in the estimate. Nevertheless, distant landmarks and an efficient compass emerge once more as the cues most likely to lead to an improvement. The similarity to the conclusion for birds is striking.

Another striking similarity is the influence of distance on the accuracy of homeward orientation in the Manchester experiments and in birds (Fig. 7.9). The effect found in birds, in which there appears to be a zone of disorientation about 40 km from home, has been interpreted as indicating that at this distance they switch from a navigational system based on familiarity to a system based on a grid-map (Matthews 1968). An alternative suggestion is that such an effect would be characteristic of a navigational system based on the detection of the compass shift of distant landmarks (Fig. 7.10).

When the change in accuracy for humans is analysed it is found that the critical factor is indeed the visibility of distant landmarks. In the Manchester

Table 7.1 Effect of cues used on the increase (+) or decrease (−) in accuracy of homeward orientation when the blindfold is removed: Series I and III, visual versus written or verbal blindfold estimate

Cue(s)	Number of individuals		χ^2	Improvement (+) Deterioration (−)
Distant landmarks and compass				
combined	13	7	1·800	+
Distant landmarks alone	10	8	0·222	+
Compass alone				
Sun	20	36	4·571	−*
Wind	9	12	0·429	−
Bright sky	5	7	0·333	−
Near landmarks	21	28	1·000	−
Familiarity	5	12	2·882	−
Guess	26	45	5·085	−*

* $P < 0.05$

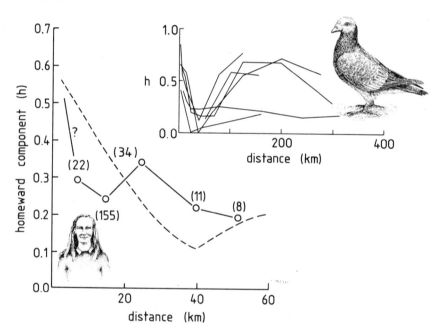

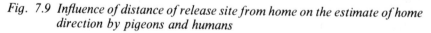

Fig. 7.9 Influence of distance of release site from home on the estimate of home direction by pigeons and humans

Inset shows the variation in homeward component of initial orientation of pigeons with increased distance of release. In the major diagram, the mean for all these lines over the first 60 km is shown by the dashed line. Dots and solid lines show the homeward component of the visual estimates of home direction by humans (Series I and III). Numbers in brackets show number of individual estimates on which each homeward component is based.

(contd. on p. 75)

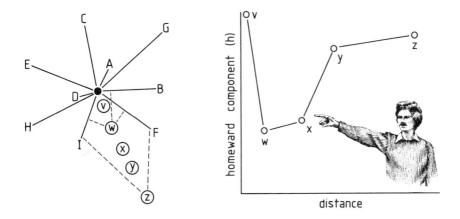

Fig. 7.10 Influence of using landmarks for location-based navigation on the
scatter of disappearance directions
(Simplified from Baker 1978)

region, the key landmarks are the Pennine Hills to the east and north (Fig.
3.7). Figure 7.11 shows that as long as these landmarks are visible in the
distance, homeward orientation is relatively accurate. Absolute visibility has
relatively little effect, except in the special case that hills can be seen *not* to be
present in the north. The confirmed absence of a particular landmark can be as
valuable in location-based navigation as the confirmed presence. Only
uncertainty is confusing. When the effect of distance on homeward orientation is re-analysed in terms of the visibility of distant landmarks, the original
relationship can be seen to disappear (Fig. 7.12). It is not distance but the
availability of familiar landmarks on the visual horizon that is critical. So, if
this is the case, what is it for pigeons that is so special about a distance of
40 km? It so happens that this is roughly the distance of the horizon features
visible from the loft. When released among these landmarks their use as
directional cues may be reduced, as found for humans (Fig. 7.11).
Unfortunately, humans have not yet been released beyond 52 km to determine
whether accuracy increases once more as it does for pigeons. Whether the
increase in accuracy with further increase in distance in birds is due to their
switching to a grid-map, to the increase in accuracy that comes from being
able to orientate to familiar landmarks from their other side (Fig. 7.10), or to
the animals' switching completely to route-based navigation and not reassess-
ing their estimate by location-based navigation, remains to be determined.

Inevitably, some of the subjects in the Manchester experiments were
released at sites that, once they removed their blindfolds, they recognised as

*(Pigeon data re-drawn from Schmidt-Koenig (1979) (after Wallraff, Graue,
Schmidt-Koenig, and Matthews) but excluding data for Ithaca pigeons from
Keeton (discussed by Schmidt-Koenig (1979) and Baker (1978)*

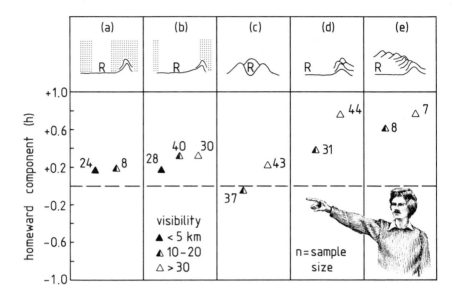

*Fig. 7.11 Influence of absolute visibility and visibility of distant (from home)
landmarks on the homeward orientation of humans in the Manchester
region (Series I and III)*

(a) Poor visibility, no distant landmarks visible
(b) Presence of distant landmarks distinguishable only with difficulty
(c) Distant landmarks obscured by topography of release site
(d) Distant landmarks visible to east but not to north
(e) Distant landmarks visible to east and north

being familiar to them. Figure 7.13 compares the performance of these
subjects, released within their familiar area, with those that were released
beyond their familiar area but within their familiar area map. It can be seen
that in most situations those within their familiar area had little if any
advantage over the others. The one exception occurred when visibility was
reduced so that only near-distance landmarks could be seen. Under these
conditions, subjects within their familiar area, being able to recognise
direction from familiar nearby landmarks, performed far better than those
that could not. As well as emphasising the occasional advantage of pilotage
over navigation, this again emphasises the importance of distant, horizon
features in location-based navigation.

It is considered that all releases in the Manchester series were within the
familiar area map of the subjects in that, except in mist, the Pennines were
either visible or their absence could be confirmed. Experiments on the
carnivorous leaf-nosed bat, **Phyllostomus hastatus**, in Trinidad also suggested
that homeward orientation was much reduced when a familiar range of hills
was no longer visible (at night) on the distant horizon (Williams and Williams
1970). Rarely, for other animals, is it possible to know whether any given

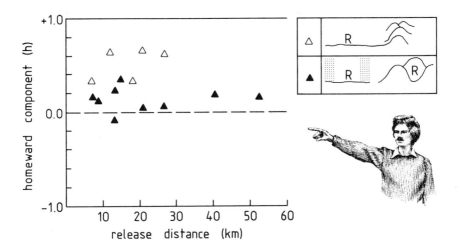

Fig. 7.12 Lack of influence of release distance on homeward component when analysed according to visibility of distant landmarks (Series I and III)

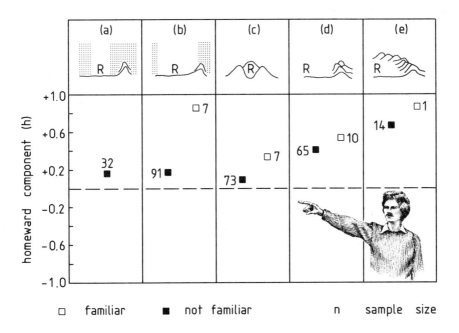

Fig. 7.13 Influence of familiarity with release site on homeward component when analysed in relation to visibility of distant landmarks (Series I and III)

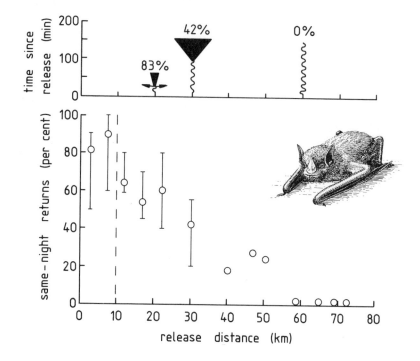

Fig. 7.14 Influence of release distance on behaviour and homing success of the carnivorous leaf-nosed bat, Phyllostomus hastatus, *as determined by radio-tracking*

Bats were taken from roosts in the limestone caves of the northern mountain range of Trinidad, ☿, mean per cent homing success of bats ± range in different experiments. Vertical dashed line, limit of normal foraging range. In the upper diagram, waved line shows period of search before setting off in straight flight. Black sector, range of departure directions. Percentage of individuals that have homed successfully after the time indicated is shown. The mountain range in which the roosts were located could probably have been seen by the bats: clearly from 10 to 20 km; with difficulty from 30 km; and not at all from 60 km.

(From Baker (1978) after Williams and Williams)

release site is within or beyond the limits of the animal's familiar-area map. It has been suggested (Baker 1978, 1981a) that most authors tend to under-estimate the size of the familiar-area map, often confusing it with the familiar area. This is true even with respect to visual landmarks. As far as pigeons are concerned such underestimation is even more likely if it is found that they can make use of infra-sound landmarks.

Kreithen (1978) has demonstrated that birds are capable of detecting the very low-frequency infra-sounds (0·1–10·0 Hz) given off by ocean waves and major topographical features such as mountain ranges. It is not yet certain, however, that birds can determine the direction of such features. If they can, it means they can add to their mental map acoustic landmarks thousands of kilometres away. It would then be certain that hardly any pigeon releases have occurred beyond the boundaries of the familiar-area map. For the moment, however, it is perhaps safest to assume that a bird's familiar-area map is limited by the furthest visual or olfactory landmarks with which it is familiar.

Nevertheless, it seems likely that relatively few releases have been beyond the limits of a bird's familiar-area map, and even these have taken no account of the possibility of route-based navigation. As a result, there is no critical evidence to demonstrate whether pigeons have access to a grid-map or to long-distance gradients. Few workers active in the field now believe that birds have access to the most likely of all grid maps, that based on the sun's arc, though it should be said that attempts to discredit grid maps are as open to interpretation in terms of route-based navigation as are attempts to support such maps.

The evidence against Matthews' sun-arc hypothesis has been summarised by Schmidt-Koenig (1979). Briefly, experimenters have attempted to disrupt a bird's ability to assess the sun's altitude and how far along its arc it has travelled. This has been done by altering the sun's apparent position with mirrors or by clock-shifting the bird (Fig. 7.15) so that it misinterprets the sun's position on its arc. In no case has it been found possible to shift the bird's homeward orientation in a way consistent with the use of a grid map based on the sun's arc. The only positive evidence for one of the coordinates, that of latitude, was provided by Whiten who showed that, when restrained in a box, birds may be able to monitor the sun's altitude and to use this to assess displacement. In all other cases, the pigeons have not been disoriented except in the sense that clock-shifting alters the bird's sun compass (Fig. 7.15). However, it could be argued that with their grid map distorted, the birds determined home direction solely by route-based navigation.

For birds, therefore, there is no real evidence for (or against) the existence of grid maps. For humans without instruments there is similarly no evidence for the existence of grid maps. The nearest to such a mechanism is the use of zenith stars deduced by Lewis (1972) to have been used by the island navigators of Polynesia, though there are no known cultures that still use this method. Moreover, even zenith stars provide only one coordinate, that of latitude, toward a grid map.

Stars stay in the same position of the sky relative to each other but the whole rotates around an imaginary axis, marked in the northern hemisphere by Polaris, the pole star. Stars keep to the same path throughout the year, each always rising at the same point on the horizon. As the Earth rotates, each star appears to come up over the eastern horizon at its own special point, describes its arc across the sky, and sets on its westerly bearing. As it progresses from east to west it passes directly above all places with the same latitude. A knowledge of which stars pass directly overhead at the required destination (e.g. Sirius passes directly overhead at Vanua Levu, Fiji Islands) would be useful in navigation. By itself, however, it would not be enough. A person can keep travelling until he finds that the same star passes overhead (i.e. is a zenith star) as at his required destination. He then knows that he is at the correct latitude. He does not know, however, whether he is east or west of the destination, nor how far. For this a knowledge of time is necessary: whether

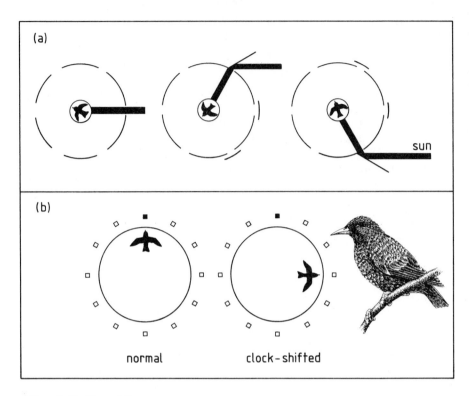

Fig. 7.15 Use of the sun as a compass

(a) Starlings were placed in an orientation cage in a circular room with six windows. When exposed to direct sunlight, the starlings oriented to the northwest. When the apparent position of the sun was shifted by a combination of shutters and mirrors, the starlings changed their compass orientation accordingly.

(b) Starlings are trained to feed from a pot in a fixed compass direction using the sun as a compass. They compensate for the movement of the sun across the sky during the day and continue to feed from the same pot. When exposed to an artificial day/night regime with light-on and light-off 6 h behind natural sunrise and sunset, and then placed back in their cage, they feed from a pot in a compass direction 90° clockwise from that to which they were trained. This shows: (1) the birds are using a sun compass; (2) they compensate for the sun's shift across the sky using their sense of time; and (3) they use the light/dark interphase as a means of setting and phasing their internal clock.

(From Baker (1978) after Hoffman and Kramer)

Fig. 7.16 Star maps of the northern and southern skies showing the features referred to in this and later chapters

Dotted outline indicates the Milky Way. Stars on the celestial equator pass directly overhead all points on the equator of the Earth.

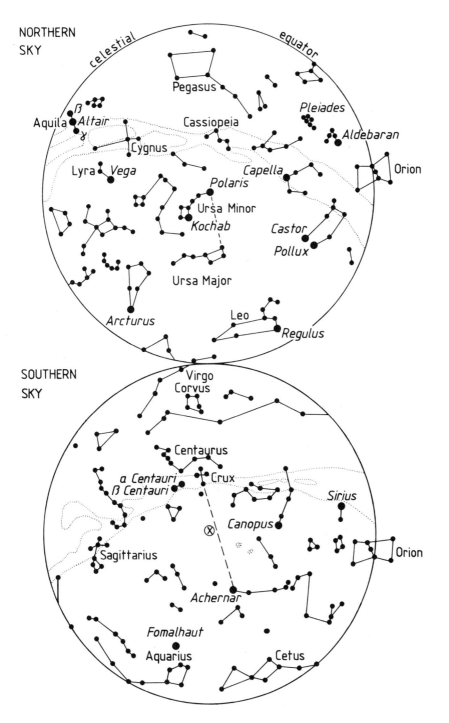

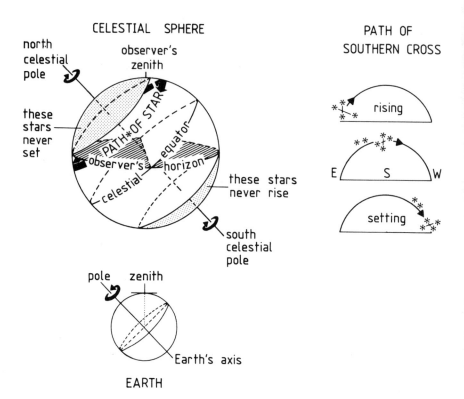

Fig. 7.17 *Apparent rotation of the night sky as caused by the rotation of the Earth*

Stars always retain the same positions relative to one another but appear to move across the sky, rotating about the north and south celestial poles (axes of rotation). As viewed from the equator, for example, the constellation of the Southern Cross, along with its two 'pointer' stars of α and β Centauri, rises on its side in the east, is more or less vertical when due south, and sets on its side in the west.

the star passes overhead at the destination before or after, and by how much, it passes over the present position.

Zenith stars are useful, therefore, only if the navigator knows by some other means whether he is east or west of home. It seems likely that the island navigators of Polynesia, knowing the direction of their destination before setting out, deliberately aimed to strike the correct latitude to one side of the destination, usually to the east (i.e. windward and upcurrent). They then turned west and completed the journey with minimal effort (Lewis 1972). There is no indication, therefore, that Polynesians, nor any other humans, before the advent of instruments, made any use of a true bicoordinate grid map. We may doubt, also, that such a map is used by birds.

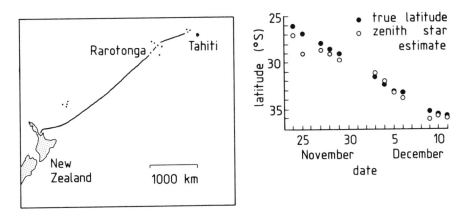

Fig. 7.18 The use of zenith stars to determine latitude

Having grasped the principles of Polynesian navigation techniques, David Lewis set off by catamaran to travel, without instruments, from Tahiti to New Zealand. The ship's company consisted of Lewis, his wife, their two daughters (then aged 3 and 4) and Priscilla Cairns, an experienced navigator. Priscilla Cairns had instruments and kept a log of the journey for comparison with the estimates being made by Lewis without instruments. Comparison took place only once the journey was completed. The graph compares Lewis' estimates of latitude during the journey, using the zenith star technique, with latitude as determined by instruments.

(Compiled from Lewis 1972)

Our review of experiments on the navigation of humans and other animals has suggested that all explorations have to be achieved entirely by a combination of route-based navigation, using a variety of cues, and location-based navigation, using only a familiar-area map. In the next chapter we can use this and other information to reconstruct the mechanisms used by humans and other animals in natural exploration, outside of the experimental situation. The role of the magnetic sense is considered last of all in this reconstruction. Indeed, it is discussed in a separate chapter (Chapter 9) once the wider navigational perspective has been established.

8

Aborigines, Polynesians and city dwellers: exploration and navigation in action

'I don't go far in the beginning; I go some distance and come back again, then, in another direction, and come back, and then again in another direction. Gradually I know how everything is, and then I can go out far without losing my way.' Thus an anonymous Australian aborigine described (in Gatty 1958) the way he built up his familiar area during 'walkabout', that period of adolescence during which young males go solitarily out into the bush for several years and finally graduate in the art of survival and navigation. Training in tracking animals and pathfinding begins as soon as the child leaves his mother's cradle (Magarey 1899) and the young child, by accompanying the family group on their wanderings, will already have built up a large familiar area. Not until adolescence and walkabout, however, does the young male explore solitarily over any distance. According to Howitt (1873), the aborigine's ability to find his way over such large inhospitable areas depends entirely on intense familiarity: special knowledge of the district belonging to his own tribe or family; general knowledge as regards the country of neighbouring tribes. He knows the land thoroughly because he was born in it and has roamed over it ever since.

Many of the people who read this book will be, or will have been, students and probably remember intensely what it is like to arrive in a new city and to be faced with the task of having to establish a familiar area and to carve out a new home range (Baker 1981a). Mainly this involves finding the best places for this or that and the best, most economical, routes to travel between them. The aborigine's description of how he establishes a familiar area could just as easily be a description of a new student's movements in an unfamiliar city. The first few weeks in a new place are ones of intensive exploration. Eventually, exploration slows down as the familiar area and home range become established, though it continues at a low rate throughout the three years or so spent in the adopted city. Few people are aware of the process by which they become able to find their way around their city with ever-increasing efficiency. Baumgarten (1927) stressed the importance of adopting fixed, major reference points but also showed how, in the early stages, it is possible to be disoriented if the city is then approached by an unfamiliar route. The ploy of travelling in different directions, to become familiar with the appearance and relationships of landmarks as seen from different angles, is as important to the city dweller as it is to the aborigine.

The city dweller does, however, have a major advantage over the nineteenth-century Australian aborigine. More important than maps and

Fig. 8.1 Australian aborigine, Arnhem Land
(Photo courtesy of Axel Poignant)

place-names is the ubiquity of people from whom navigational information can easily be obtained by inquiry. This is not to say that social communication was not also important for non-industrialists. The role of communication in the exploration of the North American Indian was clearly described by Colonel Dodge in his book *Our Wild Indians* (Dodge 1890).

Ask a nineteenth-century Amerindian how to go to a place one kilometre or a hundred kilometres away and he simply pointed out the direction. Press him closely and if he had been there he would describe in minute detail the landmarks by which to navigate. Similar and monotonous as they may appear to a stranger, each hill and valley, each rock and clump of bushes, has its own distinguishing feature which he could describe. When a group of young men wished to go on a raid into unknown country, it was customary for the older men to assemble the youngsters for instruction a few days before the fixed time for starting. An old guide, Espinosa, who had been a boy-prisoner among the Comanches, described the method of instruction to Dodge. When all were seated in a circle a bundle of sticks was produced, each one marked with notches to represent the days. Starting with the stick with one notch, an old man would draw on the ground with his finger the first day's journey. Rivers, streams, hills, valleys, ravines, hidden water-holes were all shown in relation to prominent and carefully described landmarks. When all understood the first day's journey, the first stick was put away, the stick with two notches taken out, and the second day's journey drawn. And so on until the end. Espinosa described one party of young men and boys, the eldest not more than nineteen years. None had ever been to Mexico. Yet they set out from the main camp on Brady's Creek in Texas to make a raid into Mexico as far as the city of Monterey (an air-line distance of over 600 km) solely from the information represented and fixed in their minds by these sticks.

Communication from one to the other was therefore important to pre-industrialist Man, but it was not the total answer to exploration and navigation. It was of little use for people exploring in regions unknown to any of their acquaintances. Gatty (1958) has suggested that exploration was seldom, if ever, completely into the unknown; that always there was a goal of some sort, even if that goal was a fabled goal, not a real one. The history and folklore of western Europe, particularly Ireland and Portugal, is full of mythical islands which supposedly lie to the west in the Atlantic Ocean and which were the cause of many voyages of search. Gatty further theorises that oceanic explorers often came to suspect that land lay in a particular direction from observing the oversea migrations of land birds. He suggests that season after season the Polynesians, for example, watched bird migrations and once they were convinced they had found a consistent route they set out to follow it. Thus the discovery and colonisation of New Zealand by first the Polynesians from settlements around the Solomon Islands and then, about 650 years ago, by the Maoris, from Tahiti, could have been based on observation, respectively, of the overseas migrations of the Shining Cuckoo, **Chalcites lucidus**, and Long-tailed Cuckoo, **Eudynamis tahitensis.**

Although there is some advantage in not departing on a long sea journey without good reason to believe there is land at the end of it, this is less pressing overland. At the level of the individual, over relatively short distances, it seems likely that a great many explorations are initiated into unknown country, simply to see what is there. It is through individuals of first **Homo erectus** and then early **Homo sapiens** exploring a few kilometres into the unknown, generation upon generation, that Man emerged from his African cradle and spread across all the habitable land of the Earth. Even now, every human individual at some time in their life is likely to explore simply for the sake of finding out what some unknown (to them) region has to offer.

In previous chapters we concluded from experiment that, during exploration, navigational technique involves a combination of route-based and location-based mechanisms. The route-based element involves monitoring the direction of travel and relative distance during the different stages of the journey. The location-based element involves a check of position and direction in relation to distant, recognisable landmarks. The means of monitoring direction used by non-industrialist explorers, as well as more recent ones, have been reviewed by Gatty (1958). Unlike birds, it is rare for earthbound creatures such as Man to find that the quickest and easiest route between any two points is a straight line. Normally, the most economical path involves detours which have to be assessed. Moreover, as far as possible, each stage of the journey, including detours, should be a straight line. As every marine navigator knows, and land navigators soon learn, curves are notoriously difficult to monitor.

The first step in exploration, therefore, is usually to set off in a straight line, and to make detours where necessary also as a succession of straight lines. In open, treeless countries, the common practice is to find two landmarks ahead and line them up, and to do the same looking back. Back marks are just as important as fore marks for they double the distance over which location-based navigation can take place during the return journey. In the absence of natural back marks, Man can make his own. In Australia, the aborigines light fires of Spinifex plant in open country and keep the smoke from these in line as they move on. Fires, however, are relatively temporary, though the remains of a fire can serve as a trail marker on subsequent journeys. One of the simplest, relatively permanent, and most frequent trail-marker and back-liner used by Man is the cairn, heaps of rocks built by the explorer in a pattern recognisably different from any natural formations. The steppe nomads of Mongolia still make use of hilltop cairns (Caroline Humphrey, personal communication). So, too, did Antarctic explorers, though in their case the cairns were of snow and ice, not rocks.

Fig. 8.2 Tundra nomads, Mongolia
(Photo Brian Moser/Granada T. V./Alan Hutchison Library)

Such artefacts are rarely possible on water, though in the sheltered inlets of the coast of British Columbia, the Amerindians dropped cedar chips from their boats on fishing trips, thus marking their route in times of thick fog. In forests, also, long-distance markers are of little use and all woodsmen seem to have devised methods of trail-blazing, breaking branches and hacking marks on trees with a hatchet or knife. Often direction was indicated by making one gash on the front of a tree and two on the back and by breaking a branch in the direction of a turn or detour. The Amerindians of the eastern United States deformed the trees permanently in the direction of the trail by pulling a branch away from the horizontal and tying, or staking, it in position. In time the branch grew vertically from the point where it was tied. Many of these, marking nodal positions and important detours on the Amerindian's regular routes, still exist and at places in Illinois, the Mississippi Valley, and Pennsylvania are preserved as historic landmarks. Even in forests, however, distant landmarks were important to the trail-blazing explorer who at intervals had to climb a tall tree to check his line.

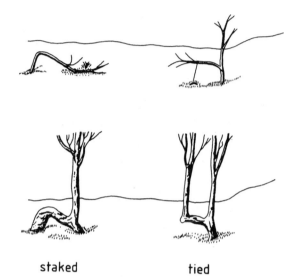

staked   tied

Fig. 8.3 Two forms of Amerindian trail marker
(Drawn from descriptions and diagrams in Gatty 1958)

In the absence of distant landmarks, whether natural or man-made, the land may still provide directional information. The alignment of ridges of dunes, sand ripples, or snow ridges in accordance with the prevailing wind has already been mentioned. Gatty (1958) describes various other cues available to the trained eye that result from the combined action of wind and sun on soil, rocks, and in particular on the vegetation. The shape of trees, the growth of lichens, or simply the species of plants growing on different sides of a valley, can all indicate compass direction. So, too, can the direction of flow of rivers and streams. As hill and mountain ranges are often linear, drainage systems tend to flow in a common direction over quite large areas.

The role of similar navigational information, so important in human navigation and exploration, has largely been overlooked for other animals. Yet such tantalising glimpses as we have suggest that such clues are as important to other species as to Man. The probable use of distant landmarks by Homing Pigeons was noted in the previous chapter. The fact that Caribou,

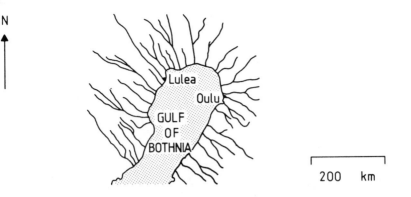

N

200 km

Fig. 8.4 In many regions rivers over a large area flow in a common direction

Rangifer tarandus, and Wildebeest, **Connochaetus taurinus**, make use of natural leading lines such as rivers, valleys, frozen lakes, and ridges during their seasonal migrations suggest that they too have a mental map of the lie of the land. Lemmings, **Lemmus lemmus**, when crossing ice-covered lakes, orientate toward the mountains on the opposite side. When some salamanders are displaced experimentally, they show, before beginning to set off toward home, an increased rate of climbing vegetation, perhaps better to sample distant olfactory landmarks and wind direction. Many large mammals use well-worn trails, particularly through woodland, during their seasonal migrations. These often result simply from repeated use, but many carnivores, for example, also make marks on trees with their claws. Other mammals mark trails by depositing scent, faeces or urine. Such trail marks convey a wealth of information to other individuals, particularly explorers, and undoubtedly serve also to deter them from exploring the area further (Baker 1978, 1981a). So too, of course, did the trail marks made by humans. Small mammals, although they almost certainly climb vegetation occasionally to sample distant visual and olfactory landmarks, establish relatively permanent runways along the routes that they eventually adopt. Banding recoveries of bats have shown strikingly the way some species make use of river systems and rows of hills and mountains during the outward phase of their explorations, and the often inferior homing performance of Pigeons from the Freiburg loft in Germany shows some indication that the birds have learned their loft is in a city on the edge of high ground to the east of the Rhine but have some difficulty in recognising the correct area.

In the face of such a wealth of navigational information available to Man and other animals from the land, it seems at first sight almost superfluous to suggest a role for celestial cues (sun, moon, stars), a wind compass, or the Earth's magnetic field. Nevertheless, such 'compass' cues play a vital role in the navigation mechanisms of all animals, including Man. Stars, in particular, provide a wealth of information (Figs. 7.15 and 7.16).

In effect, stars act as long-distance landmarks and provide three main sources of information. First, there is the zenith star phenomenon described in Chapter 7. Second, the night sky has a fixed axis around which it rotates during the course of the night and with the seasons. This axis of rotation

*Fig. 8.5 Wildebeest (top) and Caribou often follow topographical features
such as ridges and lakes during their seasonal migrations*

*(Wildebeest photo by Norman Myers, courtesy of Bruce Coleman Ltd. Caribou
photo by Frank Banfield, courtesy of the Canadian Wildlife Service.)*

marks the direction of due north in the northern hemisphere and due south in
the southern. Thirdly, at any particular place, the same star sets at the same
position on the western horizon night after night throughout the year, though

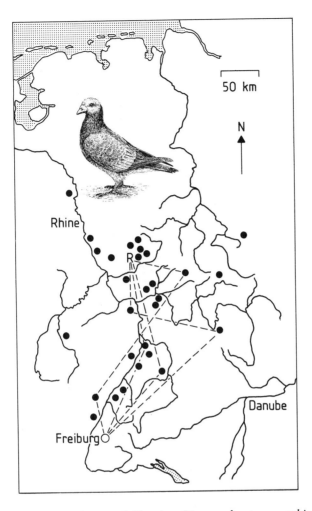

Fig. 8.6 Apparent confusion of Homing Pigeons by topographical features

Birds from the Freiburg loft, released at R, show a clear association between recovery locations and the edge of high ground

(From Baker (1978) after Pratt, Wallraff and Fullard)

four minutes earlier each night. Similarly, over the eastern horizon, individual stars always rise at the same position, again four minutes earlier each night.

Probably all human cultures have noticed and made use of the axis of rotation of the night sky as a long-distance landmark. Unlike topographical landmarks, this axis stays in the same direction and is not eventually overtaken, needing to be substituted by some other landmark. Only trans-equatorial migrants encounter any difficulty, having to switch from the northern to the southern axis of rotation. At the equator the two axes sit on their respective horizons. Polynesians made use of the axis of rotation. So, too,

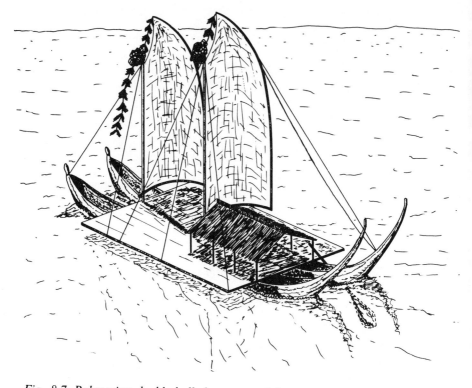

Fig. 8.7 Polynesian double-hulled canoe used for long sea journeys

did the Arabian marine navigators (Gatty 1958) and probably all other human cultures, on land and sea. So, too, do birds.

Emlen (1972) carried out experiments in a planetarium, on Indigo Buntings, **Passerina cyanea**, and found, using an orientation cage, that his birds could orientate to the night sky. Experiments on hand-raised birds showed they were not born with a mental map of the stars but were predisposed to learn star patterns during their first few weeks of activity. Their main requirement to be able to use the night sky was that during their first few weeks, the sky rotated about an axis. At the end of this period, however, the birds could identify the axis under even a stationary sky. Next, by blacking out different parts of the planetarium sky and noting when individuals were disoriented, Emlen found that different individuals were using different star patterns as pointers but that all were inclined to use stars within 15° of the axis. The natural star patterns were unimportant and by changing the position of the axis or by using a completely fictitious pattern of points of light, Emlen could show that the birds were still able to find and use the axis for orientation.

The major basis of the Polynesian system of navigation is the use of horizon stars. Essentially, orientation is maintained to setting or rising stars as they approach or leave the horizon. Some allowance has to be made for the stars not descending or rising perpendicularly, otherwise the mechanism is straightforward. As the night progresses, individual stars set but as this happens the navigator simply transfers to the next star up that is taking the same path. A sequence of five or so stars is sufficient to maintain orientation in a particular direction throughout the night. Most human cultures have probably made use of horizon stars, though in cloudier latitudes than Polynesia the mechanism may not have been the most important. There is no evidence for or against birds making use of horizon stars.

Birds and Man are not the only animals known to use stars. Bovet (1968) has shown that Deermice, **Peromyscus maniculatus**, orientate at night, almost certainly by the stars, and amphibians also can use the night sky to orientate, again probably by use of the stars (Ferguson 1971). There is strong circumstantial evidence that the Large Yellow Underwing Moth, **Noctua pronuba**, also orientates by the stars, with patterns on the celestial equator (Fig. 7.16) being implicated (Sotthibandhu and Baker 1979). In the case of this moth, however, which is using the stars for orientation, not goal orientation, there is no attempt to compensate for the stars' movement across the sky during the course of the night and the moth's compass orientation changes by about $16°$ per hour.

A multitude of animals, both vertebrate and invertebrate, have been shown to use the sun for orientation. Again animals such as butterflies (Baker 1978) and crabs (Rebach 1978) do not compensate for the movement of the sun across the sky. Most demonstrations, however, have been of the use of the sun as a compass; for this it is necessary for the animal to take into account the sun's movement and to compensate for it (Fig. 7.15). Many animals, from Homing Pigeons to Honey Bees, have been shown able to do this. Birds, when tethered, have a sun compass accurate to within $±3·4–5·1°$ (McDonald in Schmidt-Koenig 1979). In the tropics, Honey Bees can determine direction at all times except those few minutes each year that the sun is within $2°$ of the zenith (Frisch 1967).

The prime requirement in compensating for the sun's movement is a sense of time. It has long been known that internal clocks with an accuracy of within $0·3$ per cent are widespread among animals (Rawson in Barlow 1964). Lewis (1972) carried out an experiment in the catamaran **Rehu Moana** in which he sailed 3600 km in three 'legs' across Polynesia from Tahiti to New Zealand (Fig. 7.18) using only the ancient navigational techniques he had learned from books. These techniques were sun and star steering and the use of zenith stars to judge latitude. No instruments were used, but on board was an experienced navigator with instruments who kept a log of the journey so that estimated and actual positions could be compared once the journey was completed. Lewis found that his estimates of time of day were generally as close as 10 minutes but were erratic and sometimes erred by an hour or more. Nevertheless, he was able to use the sun as a compass with sufficient accuracy for the last and longest leg of the journey, 2600 km from Rarotonga to New Zealand, to culminate in a landfall whose latitude was only 42 km in error.

In many ways, the sun is a more difficult and less informative navigational aid than the stars. It does not stay on the horizon, nor is there a succession of reference points as with horizon stars. The sun does not stay on a constant compass bearing like the axis of rotation of the night sky and is thus subject to any errors involved in the judgment of time. Moreover, in many parts of the world, the daytime sky is much more likely to be overcast than the night sky. It is usually thought that most birds perform their long-distance migrations at night because they are better able to avoid aerial predators and interfere less with feeding and other important activities. An additional factor could well be that, like the Polynesians, they find, or have been exposed to natural selection to use, the easier navigational guides available at night.

The sun does, however, have one advantage over the stars: it casts a shadow on the ground. This by itself allows orientation without the need to look up at the sun. There is some evidence that Pigeons, as well as Man, use the sun's shadows for orientation (McDonald in Schmidt-Koenig 1979). The moon also casts a shadow, but as in most other respects, it is less useful than the sun. Although when available the moon is used for orientation by a range of animals (e.g. sandhoppers, moths and birds—Baker 1981a), it spends a large part of a large proportion of nights below the horizon and is unlikely ever to be the sole cue used for nocturnal orientation. Its role, when available, is probably as just another, albeit more easily detected, member of the night sky.

It is not difficult for the navigator to switch from one set of celestial reference cues to another as long as the cues are continuously available. Polynesians check the position of the rising sun by the fading horizon stars in the morning and then again as day turns into night. It has also been shown for birds that the continuation of accurate orientation as day turns to night is very dependent on the absence of overcast during the dusk period (Able 1978, Moore 1978).

Having considered the role of celestial cues in orientation, the situation may seem to have reversed and all the landmark information described earlier may seem superfluous. The fact of the matter is that for greatest accuracy, landmarks and celestial cues should be combined. Celestial cues are vital in the absence of recognisable landmarks, but in one sense are more useful than landmarks even when the latter are available in that they can be used over long distances whereas landmarks are forever being overtaken. Moreover, celestial cues may still be visible in mist or forest when distant landmarks are not. On the other hand, north remains north no matter how much the explorer drifts unknowingly to the east or west. This is particularly important at sea. There is no gain in being able continuously to point north if wind and current are drifting the boat rapidly to the east or west. Even on land, a tendency to veer to the right or left may not be detected relative to distant compass cues. When distant landmarks are not available, and other cues reduced, the human inhabitants of desert and other areas employed the technique of walking in Indian file (Gatty 1958). By keeping the file straight, the person at the back could ensure that the group continued to walk in a straight line despite the tendency of the leader to veer. Where landmarks are available, however, the lining up of a succession of pairs of distant landmarks enables the explorer to maintain a track the direction of which can then be related to a celestial compass.

The greatest drawback to the use of celestial cues is that they become obscured by cloud. When this happens, the direction of exploration can often be maintained by continuing to line up distant landmarks. Unfortunately, conditions that obscure celestial cues often also reduce visibility. The lining up of available near-distance landmarks loses precision. Under such conditions, most humans seem to have switched to a wind compass or, at sea, a wave compass. The latter is more reliable and is used by Polynesians in preference to the wind, though in order to interpret oceanic waves and swells it is necessary to take note of the wind. The alignment of waves is slow to change, having an inertia that resists the much more rapid variations in wind direction. The larger oceanic swells in particular, generated by the much more regular wind fields that prevail over large parts of the world's oceans, provide a relatively stable indication of direction. As long, that is, as the navigator can separate their pattern from the much more variable swells and surface waves generated and distorted by the wind and nearby islands. Polynesian navigators develop a marked facility for sorting out the wave patterns and taking their cues from the more reliable large swells. Lewis (1972) found this facility the most difficult to acquire, perhaps in part from language difficulties, but perhaps in part because the Polynesians sense the various conflicting swells by 'feel' as much as by visual cues and calculation.

On land, however, there is no alternative during periods that celestial cues have disappeared but to use the wind (or the shape of trees, orientation of sand ridges, etc.). Gatty (1958) stresses that greatest reliability comes from checking the direction of travel of high clouds, rather than wind on the face or a finger, while celestial cues are available. When the latter disappear, orientation can then be maintained relative to the wind as long as this does not change. However, as Gatty points out, changes in wind direction can often be detected in their own right. In any particular region, winds from different directions are often characterised by particular conditions of visibility, temperature, and cloud form and cover. Sudden changes in air temperature, visibility or cloud pattern can often be used to indicate changes in wind direction that may perhaps be checked against the direction of landmarks, if these are visible and celestial cues are not. The use of wind as an orientational cue by birds was formulated by Bellrose (1972) in the early 1970s and there can now be no doubt of the matter. Radar studies have shown the way that migratory birds often wait for winds from a particular direction before setting off (Richardson 1978). Moreover, experiments on pigeons in which deflection of wind direction at the home loft has a predictable effect on initial orientation when released (Fig. 8.8), apart from their implications for olfaction, also suggest a particular facility of birds to detect wind direction and to relate this to their other compass systems.

So far in this chapter we have concentrated on mechanisms of orientation during exploration, neglecting the way this relates to returning home. The system used by humans seems to have been universal. According to Gatty (1958), as people ventured forth on explorations without instruments, they maintained a constant anxiety about their home and would often look back to see where they were in relation to their point of departure. Lewis (1972) describes the way this system was drummed into him when exploring along tortuous trails in the flat, featureless scrub of the African bush where the sun was the only external reference. At each change of direction his indigenous companions would require him to point out the direction in which their camp lay, until in a day or two he was doing this quite automatically and re-orientating 'without conscious thought' at each major twist of the trail. A long

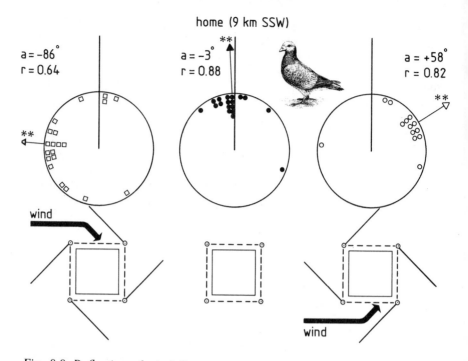

Fig. 8.8 Deflection of wind direction at the home loft influences the initial orientation of pigeons when displaced and released

(Modified from Schmidt-Koenig (1979) (after Baldaccini, Benvenuti, Fiaschi, and Papi))

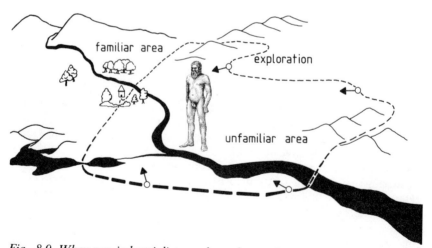

Fig. 8.9 When non-industrialists explore, they maintain a constant awareness of the direction of home

way from the African bush, in Manchester, England, a considerable proportion of students fell quite naturally into this system without, to the best of my or their knowledge, any instruction in the matter. One student described the way he imagined the University as a weight around his body, shifting position as the coach turned, now over one shoulder, now over another.

Such route-based navigation was one part, perhaps the major part, of the mechanism used by exploring humans. The other part was, at certain key positions, to relate this awareness of home direction both to the pattern of topographical landmarks and to compass direction. The final result of such exploration would be a detailed mental (familiar area) map that can be used in all subsequent movements between the places of importance within its limits. The map finally consists of landmarks, their spatial relationships, and a set of detailed instructions for movement between important sites. These instructions take the form: to reach A from B, set off northeast (or towards or away from a named horizon star or towards or away from a major landmark) for three hours, detour to the east until two landmarks are in line or one is in line with a particular horizon star, or the rising sun, etc., and then set off to the northwest.

For most human cultures we have only small pieces of the navigational jigsaw and can only surmise the way that these pieces are put together in each region to produce an appropriate and efficient local system. Perhaps only for the old inhabitants of Oceania do we have a relatively complete picture of a navigational system in action (Lewis 1972). Even this system has now died out. The islanders no longer go on long journeys by double-hulled canoes without charts or instruments. Consequently, young people no longer need to learn and develop the techniques of long-distance, natural navigation.

The Polynesians and Micronesians developed a navigational system based primarily on horizon stars. In part by individual exploration, but mainly by communication from others, the islanders learned the appropriate steering stars by which they could travel between any particular pair of islands. For example, when Lewis travelled with the Carolinian navigator Hipour from Puluwat to Saipan, he was told that the journey would be in two stages. The first was a 160 km leg from Puluwat to Pikelot, an uninhabited islet 500 m long. The second, from Pikelot to Saipan, was about 700 km, a journey of between 6 and 20 days, depending on the winds. Lewis was told that the steering stars for the first leg would be first toward the Pleiades and then, when that group had set, toward the sinking Pollux. On that occasion, Pollux set at about one or two in the morning and the journey was completed by steering at about 20° to Polaris (Fig. 8.10). This 160 km journey to a tiny islet was commonly held to be so straightforward that parties often set out for Pikelot from Puluwat on the spur of the moment when drunk on palm toddy (Gladwin in Lewis 1972). They always arrived. Once at Pikelot, Hipour pointed out to Lewis that Saipan lie in the direction of the setting Little Bear (Ursa Minor—Fig. 7.16). As a constant west-going current was anticipated on the journey, the course should have been toward Polaris, or due north. However, as there was also a strong northeast wind at the time, the canoe finally set out heading east of north by steering for the rising Little Bear. In fact, because the northern sky was obscured by cloud after sunset, Hipour had to resort to using the rising Regulus, keeping it 'before the beam to starboard'.

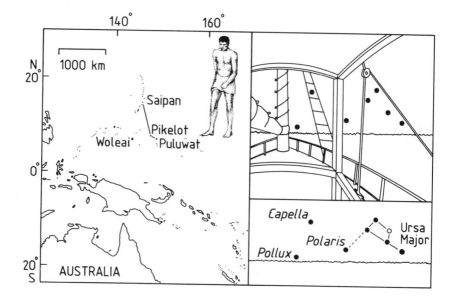

Fig. 8.10 Some of the steering stars used by Hipour during the journey from Puluwat to Saipan

(Compiled from Lewis (1972))

This example illustrates the major celestial elements in Polynesian and Micronesian navigation. Steering stars are learned along with alternatives and correction factors depending on conditions. However, this is only part of the system for, once under way, the navigator has continuously to assess how much he is being drifted by the current and by the wind. This is the process of **dead reckoning**: the estimation of position when direct measurement is impossible. Current drift or set is judged on the basis of experience of the different shapes and form of the waves depending on the interaction of current set and prevailing swell. When first setting out, some indication of the speed and direction of the current can be gained by looking back and seeing how much the starting point is shifted from alignment with the stern. Drift due to wind can be judged again by looking back and noting the angle between the wake and the orientation of the craft. From such information the navigator makes his dead-reckoning estimate of the actual direction of travel and adjusts the course to be steered accordingly. Dead-reckoning is a largely unconscious ability. In particular, interpretation of the amount of drift due to current set is based on 'feel' as much as on observation and reasoning.

Lewis found that all of the navigators with whom he had contact were able to point at any time throughout the journey not only in the direction of their home island, but also in the direction of other islands 100 km or so off their course and below the horizon. Indeed, the Micronesian system of dividing a journey into stages or *etaks* depends on being able to visualise when a particular reference island beneath the horizon is in line with a particular horizon star. There is a striking similarity between this natural element in navigation and the task that was the main element of the Manchester experiments.

The ability to visualise the apparent motion of invisible islands during the course of a journey depends as much on an ability to appreciate the distance being made good by the craft as on a mental map and on appreciation of the direction of travel. This was the least satisfactorily explained of all the features. Lewis concluded that it was judged through a multitude of indications—spray, turbulence and wind pressure among them—all processed and analysed semi-consciously in light of a vast store of experience accumulated over years of study and sea-going.

There are two further features of Polynesian navigation that facilitate safe arrival. The first is that although their island destinations may seem no more than pinpricks, they can, as targets, be expanded considerably. First, clouds, in an otherwise clear sky, can often sit unmoving above islands, increasing many times the distance from which the island's location can be detected. Second, when the sky is overcast, reflected light can often impart a green coloration to the cloud base above an island or lagoon. Thirdly, when about 30 km from the island, birds such as noddies and terns can be encountered. In the morning and evening these orient their flight paths away from and towards the nearest island. Flotsam may also appear and if there are aromatic substances on the island and the wind is in the right direction, the land may literally be smelled. Finally, within 7 or 8 km of land the waves and swell are often distorted.

The second technique used to facilitate landfall is often deliberately to bias the course to ensure that, despite any mistakes in dead-reckoning, the boat will arrive on a known side of the island, usually the windward side. In this way, once the necessary distance has been covered (or perhaps, at one time, by using zenith stars—Chapter 7) the navigator is in no doubt as to which way to turn to strike land.

Many of these elements of navigation were undoubtedly also known to other marine navigators: the Vikings, perhaps, in the North Atlantic Ocean and Arabs in the Indian Ocean (Gatty 1958). We know that the Arabs used the Pole Star, at least to measure latitude. They used the fingers of the outstretched hand to measure the height of this star above the horizon, and this angle gave them a measure of latitude. In long voyages across the Indian Ocean they used as their principal method the known directions of the winds of the seasonal monsoons. It was the Arabs, about 1800 years ago, that brought the magnetic needle from China, but it was not introduced into Europe until the time of the Crusades, long after the Vikings had rampaged the North Atlantic.

As the skies of the North Atlantic are almost chronically overcast, it is probable that the Vikings never developed a star-orientation system comparable in sophistication to the Polynesians. Their basic directions were obtained only from the sun, the directions of waves and winds, and by a knowledge of the characteristics of colour, temperature and salinity. To those that observe them, these features are as much landmarks at sea as hills and rivers are on land (Gatty 1958). Current systems sweep across vast stretches of sea, making patterns clearly distinguishable to the observant explorer. Streams of warm or

(a)

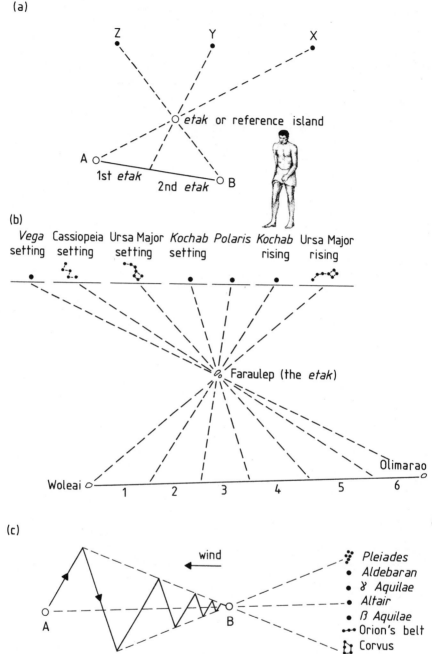

(b)

(c)

Fig. 8.11 The Micronesian etak system
The etak system depends foremost on the navigator being able to envisage the
position of islands that are beneath the horizon and to picture their movement

under the stars as the journey proceeds.

(a) A simple journey of two etaks
From island A, the navigator knows that the reference island is in the direction of horizon star X. As the journey progresses, the relative direction of the invisible reference island changes until the navigator considers that it is now in the direction of horizon star Y. This is the end of the first etak. When the reference island approaches the direction of star Z, the navigator knows that he is near island B, the destination.

(b) Woleai to Olimarao: a journey of 6 etaks

(c) The use of etak in tacking against the wind
In this, the destination itself becomes the reference island. The navigator tacks left until he considers the reference island lies in the direction of Corvus, and then tacks right until it is in the direction of Pleiades. This is repeated, producing shorter and shorter tacks as the island is estimated to draw closer.

(Compiled from Lewis 1972)

cold water carve their way between blocks of water of different temperature. Green water, nutrient rich with much suspended organic matter, is sandwiched as in a sliced cake between stretches of bluer water. Dark deep water stands out among lighter shallower water, and so on. The oceans are by no means featureless, and when all else fails, the Polynesian navigator dips his hand in the water, places it to his lips, and can judge from its temperature and/or salinity, if not precisely, at least the general area into which a particular current set or wind has drifted him under overcast skies. Bellrose (1972) has argued that the same oceanic landmarks are likely to be used by birds when migrating across large areas of sea.

The main implication of this chapter is that, throughout most of the Earth, there is no shortage of cues for natural navigation. Always some combination of compass cues and landmarks, reinforced where necessary by trail blazing and marking, allows the human navigator without instruments to monitor his explorations, find his way home, and then establish economical routes between favoured localities. In any particular instance, the difficulty if anything is in deciding which cues not to use. Against such a background the new-found magnetic sense of direction seems redundant, an impression that does little to aid its credibility. Certainly the natural navigators of the world that have been the subject of this chapter lay no claim to such a sense. If we are to accept the existence of the magnetic sense, we have to find a role for it in navigation. In particular, we need to explain that most perplexing of its characteristics: its unconsciousness. Can such an unconscious sense exist? Why should evolution favour it to be unconscious? What is its role in navigation? These are the questions discussed in the next chapter.

9

The unconscious role of the magnetic sense

So far, the human magnetic sense has been studied only in the unnatural situation of passive displacement while blindfolded. Although this has demonstrated the existence of the sense and implies a role in navigation, it does not tell us what this role may be in the normal process of sighted exploration. In the absence of direct experiment, we are forced initially to try to identify the role of the magnetic sense in our lives using indirect means. There are two ways open to us. First, we can look to other animals. Secondly, we can look to other accepted human senses, seek out which are unconscious, and gain our perspective from those.

A few colleagues have suggested to me that perhaps our lack of awareness of the magnetic sense is recent; that in modern man the sense is no longer needed, has fallen into disuse, and therefore, never develops to consciousness. This can be dismissed. The case for modern man needing to be able to navigate has already been made (Chapter 2), even though the ability may be less important than previously. Besides which, the fact that naïve students, when placed in the appropriate situation, were able to use their magnetic sense with such proficiency, suggests that they have needed to develop the sense during early life. In any case, even the experienced navigators of the world, such as the Polynesians, are not conscious of a magnetic sense. It seems, therefore, that no matter how much use of the sense is made, it remains unconscious. Moreover, the evidence for other animals suggests that in this Man is not alone.

Many people, of course, would insist that the senses of all non-human animals are unconscious; consciousness being solely a human domain. This can be dismissed (Baker 1981a). Even so, the magnetic sense does seem to be unconscious no matter which species we are discussing. The evidence for this comes from the way so many different species show a preference for information other than that derived from the magnetic field.

In the human experiments, despite an apparently high degree of proficiency at following the outward journey using the magnetic sense, there seemed a distinct tendency to abandon the magnetic field as a source of reference at the first opportunity. Only in this way can a number of anomalies in the results be explained. The subjects should have been more proficient at pointing toward home while blindfold than describing their direction in terms of north or south, etc.; yet they were not (Fig. 7.4). They should certainly not have been disoriented by poor visibility once the blindfolds had been removed (Fig. 7.11). In both cases, the subjects should have been able to use the magnetic field to point back along their outward track. The fact that they did not implies either that they could not or that the magnetic sense was passed over in favour of other information. Thus, the $71°$ rotation of estimate upon leaving the coach in Series III (Fig. 7.4) could have been due to poor vestibular inertial navigation during the short movement between the subjects' leaving their seats and disboarding. In part, also, the reduced accuracy during blindfold pointing seems to be due to an inefficient attempt to switch to using directional information gained from the feel of the sun and wind on the face. Finally, the reliance on visual cues when available even to the point of disorientation when visibility is reduced also implies an abandonment of the magnetic field when the blindfold is removed.

Humans are not alone in using several different reference systems for navigation and in switching from one to another. When studied all species are found similarly to prefer some systems or cues to others and to organise their available senses in a hierarchical way (Baker 1978, 1981a). In this hierarchy, most animals seem to prefer to use celestial cues and landmarks when these are available and relegate their magnetic sense to a lowly position. Indeed, pigeons, unless trained otherwise, often prefer to wait for the sun to reappear from behind cloud rather than use their magnetic sense alone to set off for home.

Why should animals be so reluctant to act upon information derived from the Earth's magnetic field? Local iron deposits produce magnetic anomalies that disorientate any animal relying on its magnetic sense of direction (Walcott 1978). Moreover, the sense, at least of gulls, pigeons and bees, is prone to disruption by magnetic storms in the atmosphere (Schmidt-Koenig 1979, Lindauer and Martin 1972). In many ways, therefore, magnetic fields are unreliable, more so than celestial cues when these are available. Relegation of the magnetic sense to the bottom of the hierarchy of preferences, therefore, is in accord with the rule of **least navigation** (Baker 1978): the hypothesis that in solving any particular navigational problem, animals use that subset of the information available to them that gives the best trade-off between navigational accuracy and amount of effort required to navigate.

Given that Man is not alone in preferring some senses for navigation over others and given that in all animals studied the magnetic sense comes near the bottom of the preference hierarchy, we are perhaps justified in drawing further parallels. In Man, the sense near the base of the hierarchy is an unconscious sense. Perhaps the psychological basis of the hierarchical arrangement of navigational senses is a hierarchy of consciousness. Perhaps in all animals the magnetic is the least conscious of all the navigational senses. At the very least there are no grounds for believing the human magnetic sense to be unusual in its unconsciousness. Accepting this, however, we still have to ask what roles an unconscious magnetic sense could serve. So far, only for birds among non-humans is a picture beginning to emerge.

The major initial role of the magnetic compass in birds is to set their sun and star compasses (Fig. 9.1). The European Robin, **Erithacus rubecula**, familiarises itself with the orientation of the night sky by relating it to magnetic compass directions (Fig. 9.1). In the absence of a magnetic field, the birds are slow, if not unable, to learn to use the night sky as a source of compass information. Once this has been learnt, however, the birds prefer to use the celestial information rather than the magnetic information. The same seems to

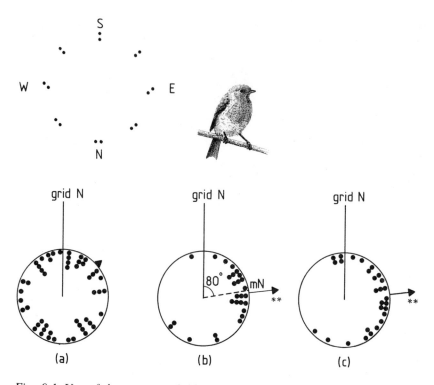

Fig. 9.1 Use of the magnetic field in setting a star compass by the European Robin, Erithacus rubecula

Robins were captured during spring migration in Spain and subjected in orientation cages to reduced magnetic fields and the artificial star pattern shown in the top figure. Both patterns were new to the birds and they were disoriented (a). The magnetic field was then reinstated but rotated by 80°. The birds adopted the traditional migration direction, toward magnetic north (b). During this period they evidently also recalibrated their star compass, adopting the artificial pattern. When the conditions shown in (a) were reinstated, the birds could now continue to orient in the appropriate direction (c).

(Compiled and modified from Wiltschko and Wiltschko (1976))

be true for the sun compass. Schmidt-Koenig (1979) has summarised the evidence which suggests that in the first instance birds learn to compensate for the sun's movement across the sky by relating its successive positions to the magnetic field. Again, however, once they have learnt it, the birds prefer to use their sun compass. There is also evidence that even experienced birds continue to compare their sun compass with their magnetic compass. Clock-shifted birds, that should misinterpret the sun's position immediately upon release (Fig. 7.15), if allowed to carry out brief training flights during their clock-shifting program, are much less likely to misinterpret the sun's direction when eventually displaced and released. Keeton and his co-workers, who carried out this work, also showed the involvement of the magnetic sense in the early stages of exploration and familiarisation. Bar-magnets attached to pigeons released under sunny conditions had no effect on experienced birds (see Fig. 6.10) but influenced the performance of birds being released for the first time.

Although caged birds can use the magnetic field to orient in the direction traditional for their long-distance migration (Fig. 6.1), the effect is weak and it is by no means clear how well seasonal migrants can use their magnetic sense in *maintaining* their migration direction over long distances. Under heavy overcast, White-throated Sparrows, **Zonotrichia albicollis**, taken aloft, released at migratory altitudes, and then followed by tracking radar, adopt meaningful headings, but less accurately than under clear night skies or sunset glow (Emlen and Demong 1978). Sinusoidal zig-zag flights become the rule compared with the straight tracks observed under clear skies. Homing Pigeons released at the site of magnetic anomalies are deflected or disoriented, but pigeons released elsewhere fly straight over such anomalies (Walcott 1978). On the other hand, magnetic storms seem to influence orientation during nocturnal migration (Moore 1977), suggesting some involvement of the magnetic sense in the maintenance of direction. Perhaps sinusoidal or zig-zag flights result from occasional checks and correction of direction of travel alternating with inadvertent veering away from that direction. This could be comparable to the tendency of humans in mist or forest or when blindfolded to veer from a straight line (Chapter 5). Perhaps a fundamental feature of the magnetic sense is that it does not allow continuous maintenance of direction. Alternatively, the human tendency to walk in circles in mist could simply reflect a lack of training of the magnetic sense. The 12-year old boy, described by De Silva (Chapter 6), who was able accurately to adopt and maintain compass directions supports this possibility. Perhaps it is only naïve humans that place less emphasis on their magnetic sense than on their equally unconscious but more idiosyncratic kinaesthetic sense (Chapter 5).

In birds, then, the main roles of the magnetic sense seem to be:

1. integration of the different celestial compass systems during early life;
2. occasional recalibration of such compass systems;
3. integration of information collected during exploration;
4. as a back-up system when other cues are unavailable.

The Barnard Castle and Manchester experiments seem to have shown that humans can also use their magnetic sense as a back-up system when they cannot see. Involvement when vision is unimpaired has not yet been studied. The magnetic sense would also seem to be ideal for maintaining continuity when switching from one orientation system to another. Still, however, none of these roles explains, for birds or humans, why the sense is unconscious. Indeed, all of the roles would seem to be more suited to a sense that is conscious at least during those periods that it is needed. All of which suggests that we have not yet found the primary role of the magnetic sense. For this, we have to look elsewhere.

The aim of exploration is to investigate the environment, look for resources, keep an eye open for danger, look for signs of other individuals, and so on. The more an animal has to concentrate on orientation and navigation, the less efficiently it can carry out these other functions. It will be common experience to everybody that they feel much more vulnerable in a strange place if they have to concentrate on finding their way around. This is particularly so when driving, but is also true when walking. There is an advantage, therefore, in a sense of direction that can function independently of the visual and other senses needed for the major functions of exploration. It is difficult to conceive of any sense that could fill such a role better than the magnetic sense, and perhaps this is its primary function: to maintain a rough sense of direction in between each conscious check of location relative to the usually more reliable visual cues. There is encouragement for this line of thought when we compare the magnetic sense with that other unconscious, but accepted, human sense: the sense of time.

The ability to judge time of day, as well as much shorter time intervals (e.g. 10 min) exists beyond doubt and is within everybody's experience. Without training, of course, the sense is relatively imprecise. Yet, as shown by Lewis during his voyage on **Rehu Moana**, the sense is or can become sufficiently accurate to be useful in navigation. In the main, it functions as a bridging system between the visually perceived times of sunrise, noon and sunset (Lewis 1972). Without doubt, however, the sense of time is an unconscious sense. Why should this be? The answer seems self-evident. If humans (or any other animal) could only measure time consciously, it would divert attention from all those other activities that are being carried out. The need is for a sense that continues to function unconsciously, but that provides an estimate when required. Even this, however, is not a conscious estimate but more a feeling for how much time has passed.

When we compare the senses of time and magnetic direction, the parallels are striking. Both are relatively crude, yet adequate. Perhaps both can be trained to greater accuracy. Certainly both are unconscious. The implication therefore is that both function to maintain continuity between conscious checks using more reliable information. Perhaps this, after all, is the primary role of the magnetic sense.

The only major difference between the senses of time and magnetic direction may concern sleep. Although there may have been natural selection for the sense of time to continue to function while asleep, for all terrestrial vertebrates, such as Man, there can hardly have been selection to maintain a sense of direction of travel while asleep, a suggestion so far supported by albeit limited evidence (Fig. 5.12).

Finally, there is some experimental evidence that a sense of direction may continue to function while concentrating on other tasks. Lindberg and Gärling (1978) in their experiments in the hospital culverts at Umeå, found no influence on ability for route-based navigation when their subjects were given a concurrent task (counting backwards) during displacement.

An unconscious magnetic sense which keeps check on the direction of travel while the navigator is concentrating on his environment could well be the basis of such dead-reckoning as that involved in the *etak* system of Micronesians (Fig. 8.11). It would be fascinating to know if helmets that rotated the Earth's magnetic field could disrupt the dead-reckoning of an experienced navigator as it does that of a naïve student. Unfortunately there are so few experienced navigators left in the world, even in areas such as Polynesia, that the chance of testing the role of the magnetic sense in the navigation of such people has virtually disappeared. The answer will have to come instead primarily from studies of modern city dwellers.

In designing such experiments, few researchers would confine their study to only one sex. Indeed, most would deliberately set out to study males and females in proportions as equal as circumstances would allow. Yet there is a feature common to most discussions of human navigation: male chauvinism. In this book, such chauvinism has carefully been hidden from all but the most observant readers. Only in Chapter 8 did the veneer of impartiality wear really thin.

Chauvinism is chauvinism, even when it is justified, and at first sight, exploration and navigation might seem to be an area where male chauvinism is so justified. Most males who read this book will, at some time in their lives, have experienced the sensation of solitary exploration over some distance. Relatively few females will have experienced this same sensation. When they have explored, females will have been much more likely to have had the company, at least of other females, and probably also of males. Perhaps this difference is less now then at any other time in human history. Until recently, however, it was extremely unusual and merited comment for a woman to be involved in long-distance exploration, even if she was in the company of males. A typical comment is that of Diaper (in Lewis 1972) who described the return to Tonga of 80 voyagers. These youths and one 'physically, perfect; morally, very imperfect' young woman had been away on a year's exploration of outlying islands, mostly Samoa.

If exploration, and hence navigation, has throughout human history been primarily a male activity, the possibility has to be considered that natural selection has favoured much greater navigational ability in males. This possibility is the subject of the next chapter.

10

Navigation by males and females

Traditionally, solitary long-distance explorations by humans are a male trait. In most cultures, females spend much of their time moving around in groups relatively near to the home base. When they do go on longer-distance explorations, it is usually in the company of one or more males. Even this may be unusual. Perhaps most often the male performs the exploration alone and only later returns to collect the female if the new-found destination seems suitable.

Time and again this pattern is found. In many African tribes, as in Australian aborigines, the solitary exploration of young males is virtually a *rite de passage* into adult life (Hance 1970). In India, as in Europe, the migration from country to town is carried out first, and primarily, by solitary males (Zachariah 1968). If females migrate, they do so usually as a member of a pair, family or group (Wyon and Gordon 1971). Even in the colonisation of large areas, such as the nineteenth-century United States, the migration stream at first has a large excess of males (Willcox 1940). Only later are some of them joined by their dependent females. The biased sex and age ratio that results is well-known to be one of the major problems confronting countries subjected to major immigration streams.

Sexual bias to exploration is an ancient characteristic. In fact, it must pre-date considerably the emergence of the human species. In most primate species the majority of males at some time during adolescence carry out long, solitary explorations. Japanese Macaques, **Macaca fuscata**, for example, may be found up to 23 km from their home troop during this period. Exploration takes place gradually, the individual travelling progressively further from its source. Except in a very few species, however, such as Gibbons, **Hylobates** spp., female primates rarely if ever show this behaviour. Indeed, many may never leave the troop into which they were born, entering into a powerful alliance with their mother and other females, many of whom inevitably are closely related. In other species, such as the Gorilla, **Gorilla gorilla**, and Chimpanzee, **Pan troglodytes**, in which the female almost always moves to another group, she does so primarily during adolescence but only when neighbouring groups actually meet one another.

Sexual differences in human exploration, therefore, have a long pedigree. Indeed, they could be part of Man's genetic inheritance, his legacy as a primate. Likely though this may seem, evidence cannot be presented to prove the point beyond doubt to those who wish to resist the conclusion. The implications that sexual differences in exploratory behaviour are genetically

Fig. 10.1 Australian Aborigine on walkabout
(Photo Courtesy of John Topham)

based are strong (Baker 1981a,b), but not unequivocal. Similarly, no conclusive evidence exists that navigational ability itself is inherited, though attempts have been made to obtain such evidence. Malán (in Howard and Templeton 1966), for example, showed 80 subjects (40 fraternal and 40 identical twins) a luminous point and then blindfolded them. After being led about the room in different directions on foot for a while, the subjects had to indicate the position of the point of light. The identical twins were more alike in their ability than the fraternal twins. Although this supports the suggestion that navigational ability is inherited, it does not prove the point. The methodology is open to the usual criticism of twin studies: that identical twins are treated more similarly by their parents than fraternal twins.

Whenever a sexual difference has been found, most spatial tests on humans, of whatever age, have shown males to be more adept than females. Lord

*Fig. 10.2 Jaf woman, member of the nomadic Kurdistan of Iraq
(Photo Courtesy of John Topham)*

(1941) tested the geographical orientation of children (173 boys and 144 girls). Among other things, she examined their ability to point in compass directions and toward distant localities, to indicate the direction of local features, to draw maps, and to maintain a sense of direction while travelling about. In an experiment similar in intent, but of much shorter distance, than the Manchester experiments, Lord drove the children at 30 km per hour round a 3 km course in the city of Ann Arbor, stopping now and again to test the subjects' ability to indicate north and the directions of the previous stopping places. Boys performed better than girls on all tests.

Similar results are obtained during the first 3 km of the journeys in the Manchester and Barnard Castle experiments (Fig. 10.3). Males just have the edge over females but the difference is not significant. This first 3 km is the map-following phase of route-based navigation (Chapter 5). At the end of this phase, however, the situation changes dramatically. Throughout the major part of the outward journey, females seem to be consistently and markedly more adept at route-based navigation than males (Fig. 10.3). There is a suggestion that over long journeys this difference may disappear but sample sizes over such distances are very small.

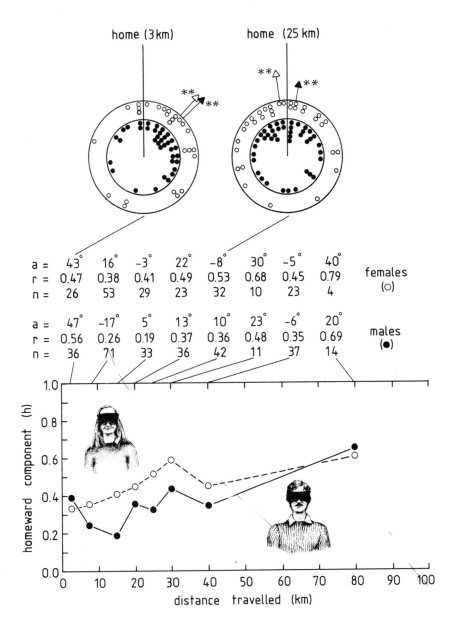

a =	43°	16°	-3°	22°	-8°	30°	-5°	40°	females (○)
r =	0.47	0.38	0.41	0.49	0.53	0.68	0.45	0.79	
n =	26	53	29	23	32	10	23	4	
a =	47°	-17°	5°	13°	10°	23°	-6°	20°	males (●)
r =	0.56	0.26	0.19	0.37	0.36	0.48	0.35	0.69	
n =	36	71	33	36	42	11	37	14	

Fig. 10.3 *Differences in ability of males and females to employ non-visual route-based navigation to monitor the outward journey as a function of distance travelled*

Verbal and written blindfold estimates lumped from Series I, II, and III. Details are given only at the 3 km and 25 km distances.

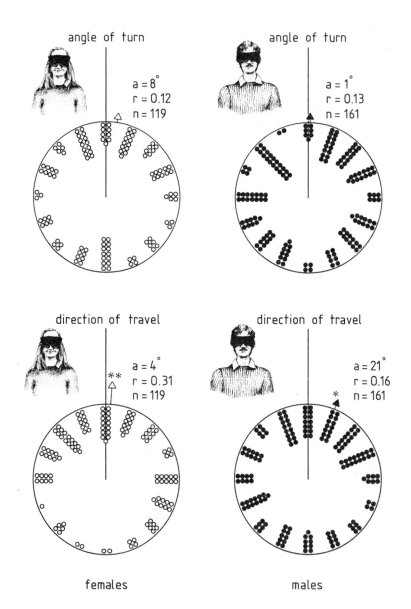

females   males

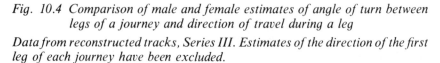

*Fig. 10.4 Comparison of male and female estimates of angle of turn between
legs of a journey and direction of travel during a leg*

*Data from reconstructed tracks, Series III. Estimates of the direction of the first
leg of each journey have been excluded.*

This greater ability of females seems to reside in a more consistent sense of direction (Fig. 10.4) rather than in any greater ability to judge angle of turn. This should imply that females have a more efficient magnetic sense than males, or at least that males place less reliance on their magnetic sense of direction. Certainly in Series II and III, the influence of magnets on the performance of males and females is always similar enough for there to be no doubt that both sexes have a functional magnetic sense (Fig. 10.5). At the same time, it has to be said that in both the Barnard Castle (Series II) and Manchester (Series III) experiments, the female response to wearing magnets seems almost always to be less extreme than that of males.

There is no apparent sexual difference in ability to point in the direction of home while blindfolded (Fig. 10.6). As soon as the blindfolds are removed, however, a significant difference once more emerges (Fig. 10.6), but now it is the males that are the more accurate. On the whole, males manage with reasonable efficiency to translate their route-based estimate into a proposed direction for travel (Table 10.1). Whether they actually improve on their route-based estimate depends on the cues used (Table 10.2). A combination of distant landmarks and/or sun compass leads to a marginal improvement in homeward orientation. The use of all other cues leads to no improvement, or even a deterioration in the estimate of homeward direction. Females, on the other hand, deteriorate significantly in their estimate of home direction once the blindfold is removed (Table 10.1). Only females that judge direction from an appraisal of near-distance landmarks (e.g. buildings, sounds or simply an assessment of location from the 'feel' of the countryside—Chapter 7) show no deterioration in accuracy (Table 10.2). The only cues which the sexes showed a difference in ability to use were distant landmarks and/or a sun compass, males being more able (Table 10.2).

The major cause of the general deterioration in the female estimates of home direction lies less in their poorer use of particular cues than in their tendency to ignore those cues that are most reliable (Table 10.3). The proportion of females that use a combination of distant landmarks and reliable compass information (sun or wind) is relatively minute, and significantly less than the proportion of males. At the same time, the proportion of females that opt to rely on intuition and simply to guess at home direction is significantly greater than the proportion of males.

The major conclusions to be drawn from the Manchester and Barnard Castle experiments are that females are more able than males at non-visual, route-based navigation but that males are more likely to reinforce their route-based estimates by location-based navigation. Moreover, males are more predisposed (whether inherently or as a result of early experience cannot be decided) to refer to distant landmarks and visual compasses. They are also better able to interpret and use this information. When females attempt to use location-based information they rely more on nearby landmark information and a general interpretation of their local surroundings.

The results are entirely consistent with the suggestion that during human, if not primate, evolution, males have been subjected much more than females to the selective pressures that act during solitary long-distance exploration and navigation. On the other hand, females seem to have a system better suited to relatively unconscious navigation over short distances.

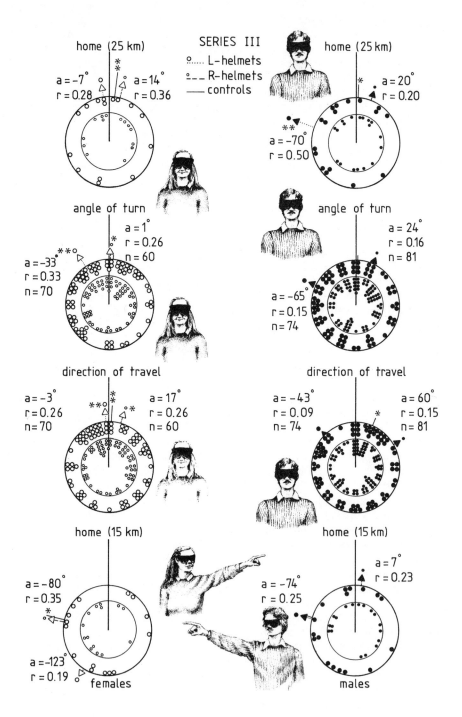

home (25 km)

a = -7°   a = 14°
r = 0.28   r = 0.36

SERIES III
○..... L−helmets
○--- R−helmets
── controls

home (25 km)

a = 20°
r = 0.20

a = -70°
r = 0.50

angle of turn

a = 1°
r = 0.26
n = 60

a = -33°
r = 0.33
n = 70

angle of turn

a = 24°
r = 0.16
n = 81

a = -65°
r = 0.15
n = 74

direction of travel

a = -3°   a = 17°
r = 0.26   r = 0.26
n = 70   n = 60

direction of travel

a = -43°   a = 60°
r = 0.09   r = 0.15
n = 74   n = 81

home (15 km)

a = -80°
r = 0.35

a = -123°
r = 0.19

females

a = -74°
r = 0.25

home (15 km)

a = 7°
r = 0.23

males

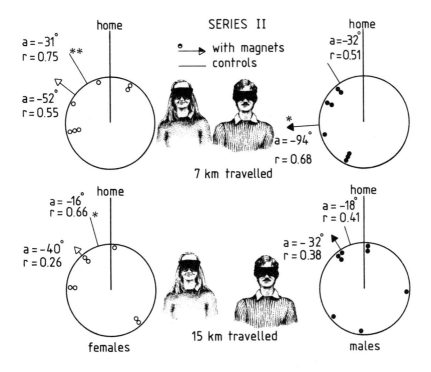

Fig. 10.5 *Comparison of response of males and females to a changed magnetic field during the outward journey (Series II and III)*

In each diagram the mean vectors without arrow heads are those for controls (individual estimates not shown). The reduced response of females suggests that for them the magnetic sense organ is nearer the periphery of the changed magnetic field. This could be due to the helmets bearing the Helmholtz coils in Series III experiments fitting males and females differently. This would not explain, however, the similar effect at the first site in the Series II experiment.

The conclusions are encouraging (or perhaps depressing, depending on point of view). They are encouraging because they suggest that navigation experiments of the Manchester type do study behaviour that is relevant to natural exploration and navigation. Yet when we consider the subtle and sophisticated landmark, celestial and other information available to humans (and other animals) during natural exploration (Chapter 8) and compare this with the limited information available during navigation experiments, we are entitled to wonder what relevance such experiments really have for the natural behaviour they attempt to mimic. This is an important question and deserves a chapter to itself.

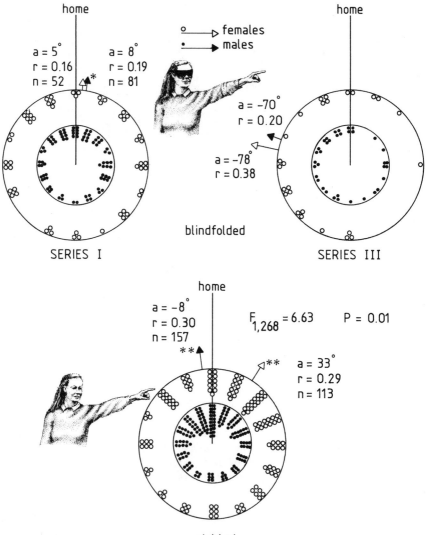

Fig. 10.6 Comparison of male and female estimates of home direction (Series I and III) as made by pointing with and without blindfolds

Sighted estimates include Series III individuals that wore activated helmets during the outward journey (see Fig. 7.7).

Table 10.1 Change in accuracy when blindfolds are removed

	sex	+	−	change	change X^2	Test for: sexual difference X^2
Visual—written/verbal	M	61	70	−	0·187	10·495** (males better)
	F	18	60	−	11·058**	
Visual—blindfold pointing	M	78	69	+	0·167	0·888
	F	64	43	+	1·703	

** $P<0.01$

Table 10.2 Use of available cues by males and females

	males use	ignore	When available: females use	ignore	used more by:	χ^2
Distant landmarks + compass	21	40	3	33	M	6·936*
Distant landmarks without compass	34	45	18	32	M	0·372
Wind compass	16	101	8	68	M	0·180
Pilotage	16	135	9	98	M	0·138
Sun compass	37	46	24	30	M	0·026
Bright-sky compass	5	41	6	29	F	0·239
Near-distance landmarks	27	108	26	72	F	1·032
'Guess'	42	109	46	61	F	5·760*

* $P < 0·05$

Table 10.3 Improvement (+) or deterioration (−) in estimate of home direction when blindfolds are removed as a function of cues used

	males +	−	When cues used: females +	−	better use by:	χ^2
Distant landmarks and/or sun compass	35	29	8	22	M	5·382*
Distant landmarks	20	9	3	6	M	2·311
Sun compass	15	20	5	16	M	1·327
'Guess'	14	20	12	25	M	0·268
Pilotage	4	5	1	7	M	—
Bright-sky compass	4	3	1	4	M	—
Wind compass	6	8	3	4	—	—
Near-distance landmarks	10	16	11	11	F	0·261

* $P < 0·05$

11

What do navigation experiments tell us?

Detailed consideration of exploration and navigation by humans emphasises above all else the tremendous range of information that is both available and used. Navigation experiments, however, strip away the senses until the human subject is left with an absolute minimum. As a result, such experiments allow a demonstration of the mechanisms that in the natural situation would be used only in the most extreme of contingencies. The multitudinous cues that normally would be used are excluded.

This is true not only for humans. Spectacular and fascinating though it may be to find that a mouse or a pigeon can still point toward home even after being displaced in a completely closed, light-tight box, the result may seem to have minimal relevance to the natural situation. Rarely, if ever, will an animal voluntarily set off on an exploration with such a paucity of environmental information. Navigation experiments are essentially attempts to replicate an exploratory journey (Chapter 2). Yet at the same time they seem to distort the information available to the animal to the point of irrelevancy. Could it be that such experiments demonstrate only an animal's ability to cope with extreme contingency, giving little insight into the mechanisms used during natural exploration?

It is right that such criticisms should be mooted, but are the points they make really so important? After all, it is the contingency mechanisms that interest us most. Few would be surprised to find that, if a pigeon or rodent is allowed to explore naturally, it will find its way around efficiently and without getting lost. Only if, like many birds or fish, it travels long distances does its navigation excite interest. The same is true for humans. In the normal way of things it is the long-distance feats of Polynesians, not the meanderings of city dwellers, that fire the imagination. Over short distances it is only the contingency mechanisms that are of great interest—the performance of humans and non-humans alike when taxed to the limit of their abilities. In particular, we wish to know whether, under such contingencies, other animals have found some navigational mechanism or principle that is beyond our human experience. Displacement–release experiments are ideally suited to a search for such ability and at first they indeed appeared to point the way to parahuman mechanisms in other animals.

The first excitement came from an apparent ability of some birds to recognise home direction from anywhere on the Earth's surface, no matter how far from home. It was this supposed ability that gave the impetus for Matthews to hypothesise the use of a grid map based on the sun's arc and for others before and after him to postulate other non-solar coordinates. Such a grid map would have been beyond the perception of any human without the aid of instruments. We can now see that the theoretical and practical search for a grid-map was probably unwarranted and that long-distance navigation by birds at release distances of hundreds or thousands of kilometres is probably dependent on route-based mechanisms. In their own right, however, even these seemed remarkable and, outside the pages of fiction, to be beyond human experience. Surprise and excitement (not to mention the inevitable disbelief) was even greater when it was demonstrated for pigeons that not only could they carry out route-based navigation but that their ability resided in a magnetic sense of direction.

In retrospect, all of this only seemed remarkable because the same experiments had not been attempted on humans. When they were, it was found not only that humans have the same facility for non-visual, route-based navigation but that this facility rests similarly on a magnetic sense of direction. At present, there is no element of the navigation system of pigeons, or any other animal, that is known to be fundamentally different from that of humans. This is not to say that other animals do not have parahuman senses. Pigeons are able to hear infra-sounds (Chapter 7) which could give them a larger familiar-area map than humans can achieve by vision. Bats use echolocation to detect landmarks near to them, but still use vision to set the limits to their familiar-area map. Amphibians use their pineal 'eye' (i.e. the light-sensitive tissue of the mid-brain beneath a translucent area of skull) to perceive the direction of the sun, but having done so use the sun as a compass in the same way as does a man. Fish undoubtedly give greater emphasis to olfactory landmarks and to the chemical signature of the water than does Man to those carried by currents of air. Fish may also use their lateral line system to build up a pressure-wave map of their surroundings. Sharks, rays and other elasmobranchs may use their electric sense to detect the Earth's magnetic field. And so on. No matter the senses used, however. Each of these animals seems to share with Man the technique of building by exploration a map of familiar landmarks that is then at the heart of location-based navigation.

If this impression of similarity is real, we may expect that all navigating animals use a combination of route-based and location-based mechanisms fundamentally similar to those used by Man. The human ego should gain encouragement from this possibility: perhaps, after all, non-human navigators do not have abilities essentially better than our own. There is, however, another side to this picture of equality, a side less flattering to the human ego. The implication can scarcely be missed that, if humans are the equal of pigeons in matters navigational, then pigeons are likewise the equal of humans. The similarities in navigational behaviour mooted in this book could have far-reaching implications for the study of animal behaviour, implications that impinge on our view of the very nature of animal behaviour. These implications are the subject of the final chapter.

12

Evolutionary implications

There was a time, not too long ago, when the cardinal sin in the study of animal behaviour was that of anthropomorphism, attributing to other animals the logic, feelings and emotions peculiar to the human condition. The determination of behaviourists to avoid committing this sin fueled the flames of ethology, that discipline that took the study of animal behaviour out into the field but sought to explain everything in terms of automatic, programmed reflexes. Feed an animal a stimulus at one point and there emerged an inflexible response at another. The past decade, however, has witnessed the behavioural ecology revolution and the attempt to develop a view of animals as sentient organisms, striving to solve the problems thrown at them by a hostile environment.

The wider context of the study of animal behaviour has left as great, if not more of, a mark on the study of animal movement patterns as it has on any other category of behaviour (Baker 1981a). Within this context, the study of migration has travelled a curious path. We have always known, of course, from subjective awareness if nowhere else, that a cerebral sense of location is a human characteristic. As such, it is just one of those cerebral characteristics, along with foresight, deductive reasoning, and language, that Man has decided set him apart from other animals. The threat of anthropomorphism led many behaviourists to seek other, more instinctive, mechanisms whereby other animals could find their way around. Moreover, for fish, birds and sea turtles at least, the search seemed partially successful. Behavioural models were developed in which the place of birth or elsewhere was irreversibly imprinted on the organism as a potential breeding site. Innately programmed orientation and other behavioural responses took long-distance migrants to traditional feeding or overwintering sites. Finally, the mysterious but instinctive mechanism of navigation guided the animal back to its imprinted breeding site. There was no need nor room in such models for a cerebral sense of location. Ethologists had successfully separated the human sense of location from that of other animals.

At the same time, the navigational mechanism itself was seen as something beyond human experience. To describe it as instinctive made it seem more rather than less mysterious and implied that it involved abilities in which Man was totally deficient. Even the proponents of a human sixth sense seemed uncertain that this was really the same as that shown by the long-distance migrants among other animals. Nevertheless, acceptance of this mysterious ability was in no way seen as a contradiction of the ethological view that the human sense of location, by its cerebral, conscious nature, was superior to that of other animals.

The implications of the review presented in this book are quite different. In accord with the new dogma of behavioural ecology, they are that there is no fundamental difference between the human sense of location and that of other animals. Although the details of the senses used may differ between vertebrates, the mechanisms of exploration and navigation and hence the sense of location are fundamentally the same no matter whether we consider a fish, a bird or Man.

As far as birds are concerned, this book has concentrated on Homing Pigeons. Only for this species are there data comparable to those now available for Man. However, Homing Pigeons, like the humans whose cities they share, live in the same limited home range each year. Other birds, the long-distance seasonal migrants, travel vast distances during the course of a year. Consider, though, the map of Oceania drawn by the Polynesian Tupaia when encountered by Captain Cook in 1769. This individual was sufficiently familiar with an area of ocean 4000 km in diameter to be able to map out nearly 80 islands and to lead Cook to 'discover' a number he would otherwise have missed. The diameter of Tupaia's familiar area map is quite comparable to that of many of the so-called 'migratory' birds. Yet it was built up by a man travelling at sea level in a canoe using the navigational techniques described in this book. Who can doubt that, using the same techniques, a bird could easily, during its first year of life, establish a familiar area map as large or larger than this simply by virtue of its greater mobility and height.

As evidence for the exploration model of bird migration grows (Baker 1981a), acceptance becomes easier that the navigational mechanisms involved are no different from those shown by other birds over shorter distances or, for that matter, by Man. It may seem a rash prediction, but perhaps, given comparable mobility, any Man could pioneer the migration routes followed annually by birds. Encouragement in such a prediction can be drawn from the example of David Lewis. Having grasped the principles of Polynesian navigation, Lewis successfully navigated his way without instruments over the 3600 km of sea from Tahiti to New Zealand in the catamaran, **Rehu Moana**.

We seem, therefore, to have reached a point in our navigational perspective at which it no longer seems strange to postulate that the natural navigation system of humans would be adequate to allow them to travel routes and distances comparable to birds. The same perspective takes us to the point where there seems no escaping the fact that birds have a sense of location comparable in every respect to that of humans. If the mechanisms of navigation are so similar, the cerebral awareness must surely also be similar. Indeed, there is no reason, beyond an unshakeable belief in human uniqueness, to search for anything but such a similarity. In which case anthropomorphism, at least as far as a sense of location is concerned, can be no longer a sin. It is just as accurate, descriptive, and meaningful to say that a bird, salamander or fish 'knows' where it is going as it moves around within its familiar area as it is for Man. As all vertebrates (at least) have been exposed during evolution to the same problems of pathfinding, it is not unreasonable that the evolutionary solution should always have been fundamentally the same. Indeed, perhaps there was a single initial adaptation in vertebrates and subsequent evolution, as sensory abilities changed to suit particular habitats, involved simply sensory variation on an original theme. In which case Man has simply inherited his sense of location and concomitant navigational mechanisms from his vertebrate ancestors. Moreover, in the same way that the broad details of this sense may be part of his vertebrate heritage, so may sexual variations in the sense be part of his primate heritage.

Such a view leads us to the heart of the great sociobiology debate that continues to rage, despite the sincere wish of many that it be allowed to die so that they may continue their studies away from the disruptive shrapnel of ideological warfare. When Edward Wilson (1975) suggested that eventually all aspects of human social behaviour would be subsumed within an evolutionary framework common to all animals, he triggered an intense reaction within the fields of sociology, anthropology and biology. So far, and not unexpectedly, debate has been waged on the battlefields of philosophy and ideology, even politics and dogma. The work on navigation, however, suggests that there may be a more profitable meeting place for studies of Man and other animals than ideological debate. Nor need this meeting place be reserved for navigation (Baker 1981a,b). If ideological differences could be set aside, there would seem to be great practical benefits to be gained from studying the behaviour of Man and other animals each in the perspective of the other. As far as navigation is concerned, it is perhaps not premature to say that experiments on humans throw into a new, much less mysterious, perspective the phenomenon of navigation as previously understood for animals such as birds. At the same time, how long would it have taken to discover the magnetic sense of humans had the study of other animals not produced a clear directive of where and how to look for it?

If we take a backward look at the sociobiology debate from the perspective of the study of animal navigation, we can see no good reason for further ideological warfare. Let us study Man and other animals side by side and let the academic and practical benefits that emerge speak for themselves.

Appendix 1.   Future work

It is my hope that this book will not only stimulate interest in the subject of human navigation but also an era of research. Doubtless most research will continue to be carried out by zoologists and experimental psychologists. There is also tremendous scope, however, for research by school teachers and clinical psychologists, having access as they do to a variety of age groups and to individuals with sensory deficiencies and brain abnormalities.

Clearly a first priority in such work is simply to replicate the Manchester and Barnard Castle experiments in a range of areas using a range of subjects rather than the specific categories of undergraduates and sixth-form students used so far. Confirmation of the magnetic effect (Helmholtz coils are most useful though for schoolteachers only bar magnets may be available) by a range of workers is also a clear priority. Doubtless, as was the case for birds, until the various people active in the field have seen for themselves that under the appropriate conditions, magnets can influence Man's sense of direction, a magnetic sense will not widely be accepted. There are still people, without direct experience, who find it difficult to accept a magnetic sense in birds, despite the wealth of evidence that puts its existence beyond doubt.

Assuming the magnetic sense in Man is confirmed, the next step is physically to locate the sense organ in the human head. Again, we now have the advantage over ornithologists in that we can begin by using the techniques and experience used in their search for the sense organ in birds. Moreover, the Manchester experiments give a clear prediction as to its position.

If it is not too late, the role of the magnetic sense in natural navigators in different parts of the world would be of extreme interest. Failing that, it is now time to determine what role, if any, the sense plays in the movements of city dwellers when vision is not disrupted. In particular, how accurately can people be trained to use this sense? Can it, for example, with training and experience, be used to correct the tendency to veer from a straight line when walking in mist or when blindfolded?

Clinical aspects could also be important. If a sense normally exists, absence of that sense may have clinical side effects. Are there people without a functional magnetic sense, either for congenital reasons or through inadvertent industrial or medical practices? If so, do such people show any clinical side effects other than a presumed loss of magnetic sense of direction? Various students during the Manchester (Series III) experiments reported side effects from wearing the helmets. Nausea, headache and disorientation were common but showed no correlation with whether the helmets were activated or not. One subject described a metallic taste in her mouth and an odd sensation around the fillings of her teeth, and this did correlate with the helmet's being activated. On the second journey of the Series III experiments, half of the controls had also been controls the previous week. The other half had worn activated helmets. There was no difference in performance of the two groups and thus no indication that the activated helmets were having any permanent influence on magnetic sense of direction. The influence of changed magnetic field on blind people who may have had the need to train their magnetic sense to a greater degree than sighted people would also be of interest.

One question always asked when I lecture or broadcast on human navigation has been whether some people are better than others, whether some people really do have a better sense of direction. This question cannot be answered from the Manchester experiments because no subject has been used more than twice as a control, but it would be of interest and would come naturally out of training programs. An associated question is how navigational ability, both route-based and location-based, varies with age in the different sexes. Do sexual differences increase or decrease with age?

Navigational performance at much greater distances than the present maximum of 52 km would be of interest for comparison with birds and to follow further the differences between the sexes. As far as comparison with Homing Pigeons is concerned, it would also be of interest to displace birds and people in the same coach to compare performance. This has already been tried at Cornell University (Keeton, personal communication) and on that occasion the pigeons performed much better, though the humans were tested only after the blindfolds were removed.

The precise mechanism by which naïve males use distant landmarks and compass cues would be of interest as would comparison with performance at such location-based navigation by both males and females following training in the craft of obtaining direction from landmarks. Finally, all experiments have so far been carried out during the day. Night-time displacements would be instructive, from the viewpoints of both route-based and location-based navigation.

Appendix 2.   Circular statistics

The questions posed by navigation experiments can only really be answered by the application of circular statistics to the data obtained. Many people not already active in animal navigation research will not be familiar with these statistics. Psychologists in particular have in the past appeared reluctant to use circular statistics, and their experiments are in consequence often difficult to interpret in the simple, most direct, sense. Rarely do they use their data to answer the simple question: have their subjects shown a significant ability to solve the navigational problems they have been set?

Anybody seriously considering experimentation on human navigation has no real alternative but to obtain copies of the publications by Batschelet (1965, 1972, 1978). There are described a wide range of parametric and non-parametric statistics to meet all contingencies. For people, such as schoolteachers, who may have difficulty in obtaining these publications and who, as a result, may be discouraged from trying experiments, I present the two simplest and most important tests that will allow them to draw some conclusions from their data. This example may also be useful for undergraduates trying to understand the analyses presented earlier in this book.

Calculation of the mean vector $(a°, r)$ (see Chapter 3, Fig. 3.4)

Usually, data are most conveniently recorded as compass angles measured clockwise from north. Care must be taken not to confuse magnetic and grid north.

Example (Fig. A2.1)

males	females
225°	135°
200°	167°
23°	90°
315°	181°
270°	140°

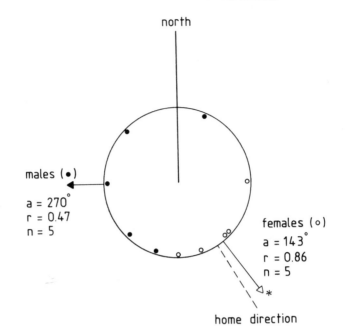

Fig. A2.1 Data used in worked example

For each angle, the cosine and sine are taken and summed:

	males		females	
	cos	sin	cos	sin
	−0·707	−0·707	−0·707	0·707
	−0·940	−0·342	−0·974	0·225
	0·921	0·391	0·000	1·000
	0·707	−0·707	−1·000	−0·017
	0·000	−1·000	−0·766	0·643
Total	−0·019	−2·365	−3·447	2·558
	V_m	W_m	V_f	W_f

Calculate $R = \sqrt{(V^2 + W^2)}$
for males: $R_m = 2·365$
for females: $R_f = 4·292$.

Calculate $\cos a = V/R$

for males: $\cos a = -0·0008$
              $a = 90°$ (as W_m is negative, $a = -90°$; i.e. $360 - 90$
              $= 270°$)
              $a = 270°$
for females: $\cos a = -0·803$
              $a = 143°$ (as W_f is positive, $a = +143°$; i.e. $0 + 143$
              $= 143°$)
              $a = 143°$

Calculate $r = R/n$

for males: $r = 2 \cdot 365/5 = 0 \cdot 473$
for females: $r = 4 \cdot 292/5 = 0 \cdot 858$

To test for a significant difference from uniformity calculate Rayleigh's $z = nr^2$
for males: $z = 5 \times 0 \cdot 473 \times 0 \cdot 473 = 1 \cdot 119$
for females: $z = 5 \times 0 \cdot 858 \times 0 \cdot 858 = 3 \cdot 681$

some critical values for z are:

n	$P = 5\%$	$P = 1\%$	
10	2·919	4·290	(adapted from Batschelet 1965
20	2·958	4·451	after Greenwood and Durand)
∞	2·996	4·605.	

The male distribution is not significantly non-uniform. The female distribution is significantly non-uniform at the 5% level.

Let the home direction be 150° (Fig. A2.1)
Relative to home direction, mean angles are:
for males: $270 - 150 = +120°$ ($+$ = clockwise)
for females: $143 - 150 = -\quad 7°$ ($-$ = anticlockwise).

To calculate V and W relative to home direction:

for males: $V_h = R_m \cos(+120°) = 2 \cdot 365 \, (-0 \cdot 500) = -1 \cdot 183$
$\qquad\qquad W_h = R_m \sin(+120°) = 2 \cdot 365 \, (0 \cdot 866) = 2.048$
for females: $V_h = R_f \cos(-7°) = 4 \cdot 292 \, (0 \cdot 993) = 4 \cdot 262$
$\qquad\qquad W_h = R_f \sin(-7°) = 4 \cdot 292 \, (-0 \cdot 122) = -0 \cdot 524.$

To calculate homeward component (h) (Fig. 3.4), $h = V_h/n$
for males: $h = -1 \cdot 183/5 = -0 \cdot 237$
for females: $h = \quad 4 \cdot 262/5 = 0 \cdot 858.$

Note: The value for h must fall within the range -1 to $+1$

In order to lump data relative to home direction simply add together the different values for each of V_h, W_h, and n and repeat the different calculations. Thus for the male and female data combined:

$V_{fm} = -1 \cdot 183 + 4 \cdot 262 = 3 \cdot 079$
$W_{fm} = \quad 2 \cdot 048 - 0 \cdot 524 = 1 \cdot 524$
$N = 5 + 5 = 10$
$R_{fm} = \sqrt{(3 \cdot 079^2 + 1 \cdot 524^2)} = 3 \cdot 436$
$\cos a = 3 \cdot 079/3 \cdot 436 = 0 \cdot 896$
$\quad a = 26°$ (clockwise of home)
$\quad r = 3 \cdot 436/10 = 0 \cdot 346$
$\quad z = 10 \times 0 \cdot 346 \times 0 \cdot 346 = 1 \cdot 180.$

The combined data for males and females are not, therefore, significantly non-uniform at the 5% level.

To test whether the mean angles for males and females are significantly different using the Watson and Williams' parametric two-sample test calculate:

$$F_{1, N-2} = (N-2)\frac{R_m + R_f - R_{fm}}{N - R_m - R_f}.$$

In this example:

$$F_{1, 8} = (8)\frac{2 \cdot 365 + 4 \cdot 292 - 3 \cdot 436}{10 - 2 \cdot 365 - 4 \cdot 292}$$

$$= 7 \cdot 708.$$

Critical values for F at different significance levels can be found in tables of the F (variance ratio) distribution, with 1 and $N - 2$ degrees of freedom. For the example given, the critical value of F at the 5 % level is 5·32. We may conclude, therefore, that males and females have significantly different mean angles, though the use of a parametric test when one of the mean angles is not significantly non-uniform is of dubious validity. In this instance a non-parametric test would have been preferable.

It should be stressed that this example gives only the recipe for calculating the various statistics. It is no substitute for a thorough understanding of the reasoning behind them and, most importantly, their limitations. For this, the reader should consult the papers by Batschelet.

References

ABLE, K. P. (1978) Field studies of the orientation cue hierarchy of nocturnal songbird migrants. *In*: Schmidt-Koenig, K. and Keeton, W. T. (eds) *Animal migration, navigation and homing.* Springer, Heidelberg. pp. 228–38.

BAKER, R. R. (1978) *The evolutionary ecology of animal migration.* Hodder and Stoughton, London.

BAKER, R. R. (1980) Goal orientation by blindfolded humans after long-distance displacement; possible involvement of a magnetic sense. *Science* **210**, 555–7.

BAKER, R. R. (1981a) *Migration: paths through time and space* Hodder and Stoughton, London.

BAKER, R. R. (1981b) Man and other animals: a common perspective to migration and navigation. *In*: Aidley, D. J. (ed.) *Animal migration.* University Press, Cambridge.

BARLOW, J. S. (1964) Inertial navigation as a basis for animal navigation. *J. Theoret. Biol.* **6**, 76–117.

BATSCHELET, E. (1965) *Statistical methods for the analysis of problems in animal orientation and certain biological rhythms.* Am. Inst. Biol. Sci., Washington, D. C.

BATSCHELET, E. (1972) Recent statistical methods for orientation data. *In*: Galler, S. R., Schmidt-Koenig, K., Jacobs, G. J. and Belleville, R. E. (eds) *Animal orientation and navigation.* NASA SP-262 US Govt. Printing Office, Washington, D. C. pp. 61–91.

BATSCHELET, E. (1978) Second-order statistical analysis of directions. *In*: Schmidt-Koenig, K. and Keeton, W. T. (eds) *Animal migration, navigation and homing.* Springer, Heidelberg. pp. 3–24.

BAUMGARTEN, F. (1927) Die Orientierungstäuschungen. *Z. Psychol. Physiol. Sinnesorg.*, **103**, 111–22.

BEISCHER, D. E. (1971) The null magnetic field as reference for the study of geomagnetic directional effects in animals and man. *Ann. N. Y. Acad. Sci.* **188**, 324–30.

BELLROSE, F. C. (1972) Possible steps in the evolutionary development of bird navigation. *In*: Galler, S. R., Schmidt-Koenig, K., Jacobs, G. J. and Belleville, R. E. (eds) *Animal orientation and navigation.* NASA SP-262 US Govt. Printing Office, Washington D. C. pp. 223–57.

BÖÖK, A. and GÄRLING, T. (1978a) Localization of invisible reference points during linear locomotion: Effects of locomotion distance and location of reference points. *Umeå Psychological Reports.* No. 139.

BÖÖK, A. and GÄRLING, T. (1978b) Localization of invisible reference points during body rotation: Effects of body rotation angle and direction of reference points. *Umeå Psychological Reports.* No. 140.

BOVET, J. (1960) Experimentelle untersuchungen über das Heimfindevermögen von Mäusen. *Z. Tierpsychol.* **17**, 728–55.

BOVET, J. (1968) Trails of deer mice (*Peromyscus maniculatus*) traveling on the snow while homing. *J. Mammal.* **49**, 713–25.

BOVET, J. (1978) Homing in wild myomorph rodents: current problems. *In*: Schmidt-Koenig, K. and Keeton, W. T. (eds) *Animal migration, navigation and homing*. Springer, Heidelberg. pp. 405–12.

CANTER, D. (1977) *The psychology of place*. Architectural Press, London.

CAVÉ, A. J., BOL, C. and SPEEK, G. (1974) Experiments on discrimination by the starling between geographical locations. *Progress Report 1973. Institute of Ecological Research. Royal Netherlands Academy of Arts and Sciences*. p. 82.

CRITCHLEY, M. (1953) *The parietal lobes*. Arnold, London.

DARWIN, C. (1873) Origin of certain instincts. *Nature, Lond*. **7**, 417–18.

DELIUS, J. D. and EMMERTON, J. (1978) Sensory mechanisms related to homing in pigeons. *In*: Schmidt-Koenig, K. and Keeton, W. T. (eds) *Animal migration, navigation and homing*. Springer, Heidelberg. pp. 35–41.

DE SILVA, H. R. (1931) A case of a boy possessing an automatic directional orientation. *Science* **75**, 393–94.

DODGE, R. I. (1890) *Our wild Indians*. Hartford, Connecticut.

EDELSTAM, C. and PALMER, C. (1950) Homing behaviour in gastropodes. *Oikos* **2**, 259–70.

EMLEN, S. T. (1972) The ontogenetic development of orientation capabilities. *In*: Galler, S. R., Schmidt-Koenig, K., Jacobs, G. J. and Belleville, R. E. (eds) *Animal orientation and navigation*. NASA SP-262 US Govt. Printing Office, Washington, D. C. pp. 191–210.

EMLEN, S. T. and DEMONG, N. J. (1978) Orientation strategies used by free-flying bird migrants: a radar tracking study. *In*: Schmidt-Koenig, K. and Keeton, W. T. (eds) *Animal migration, navigation and homing*. Springer, Heidelberg. pp. 283–93.

FERGUSON, D. E. (1971) The sensory basis of orientation in amphibians. *Ann. N.Y. Acad. Sci*. **188**, 30–6.

FISLER, G. F. (1967) An experimental analysis of orientation to the homesite in two rodent species. *Can. J. Zool*. **45**, 261–8.

FORSTER, J. R. (1778) *Observations made during a voyage round the world (in the Resolution 1771–5)*. G. Robinson, London.

FRANKEL, R. B., BLAKEMORE, R. P. and WOLFE, R. S. (1979) Magnetite in freshwater magnetotactic bacteria. *Science* **203**, 1355–6.

FRERE, H. B. E. (1870) Notes on the Runn of Cutch and neighbouring region. *J. Roy. Geogr. Soc*. **40**, 181–207.

FRISCH, K. VON (1967) *The dance language and orientation of bees*. Oxford University Press, London.

GATTY, H. (1958) *Nature is your guide*. Collins, London.

GOULD, P. R. and WHITE, R. (1974) *Mental maps*. Penguin, Harmondsworth.

GOULD, S. J. (1979) Nature seen: a natural precision engineer. *New Scientist* 446–7.

HAILEY, A. (1975) *The moneychangers*. Michael Joseph, London.

HANCE, W. A. (1970) *Population, migration and urbanization in Africa*. Columbia University Press, London.

HOWARD, I. P. and TEMPLETON, W. B. (1966) *Human spatial orientation*. Wiley, New York.

HOWITT, A. W. (1873) *in* Gatty (1958).

HUDSON, W. H. (1922) On the sense of direction. *Cent. Mag*., **104**, 693–701.

JACCARD, P. (1931) *Le sens de direction et l'orientation lointain chez l'homme.* Payot, Paris.

KAPLAN, S. (1973) Cognitive maps in perception and thought. *In*: Downs, R. M. and Stea, S. (eds) *Image and environment: cognitive mapping and spatial behaviour.* Aldine, Chicago.

KEETON, W. T. (1981) Long-distance orientation by birds. *In*: Aidley, D. J. (ed) *Animal migration.* University Press, Cambridge.

KETCHEN, E. E., PORTER, W. E. and BOLTON, N. E. (1978) The biological effects of magnetic fields on man. *Am. Ind. Hyg. Ass. J.* **39**, 1–11.

KIEPENHEUER, J. (1978a) Pigeon navigation and magnetic field: information collected during the outward journey is used in the homing process. *Naturwiss.* **65**, 113.

KIEPENHEUER, J. (1978b) Inversion of the magnetic field during transport: its influence on the homing behaviour of pigeons. *In*: Schmidt-Koenig, K. and Keeton, W. T. (eds) *Animal migration, navigation and homing.* Springer, Heidelberg. pp. 135–42.

KÖHLER, K. L. (1978) Do pigeons use their eyes for navigation? A new technique! *In*: Schmidt-Koenig, K. and Keeton, W. T. (eds) *Animal migration, navigation and homing.* Springer, Heidelberg. pp. 57–64.

KREITHEN, M. L. (1978) Sensory mechanisms for animal orientation—can any new ones be discovered? *In*: Schmidt-Koenig, K. and Keeton, W. T. (eds) *Animal migration, navigation and homing.* Springer, Heidelberg. pp. 25–34.

LEASK, M. J. M. (1977) A physico-chemical mechanism for magnetic field detection by migratory birds and homing pigeons. *Nature, Lond.* **267**, 144–6.

LEWIS, D. (1972) *We, the navigators.* Australian National University Press, Canberra.

LINDAUER, M. and MARTIN, H. (1972) Magnetic effect on dancing bees. *In*: Galler, S. R., Schmidt-Koenig, K., Jacobs, G. J. and Belleville, R. E. (eds) *Animal orientation and navigation.* NASA SP-262 US Govt. Printing Office, Washington, D.C. pp. 559–67.

LINDBERG, E. and GÄRLING, T. (1978) Acquisition of locational information about reference points during blindfolded and sighted locomotion: effects of a concurrent task and locomotion paths. *Umeå Psychological Reports.* No. 144.

LINDENLAUB, E. (1955) Über das Heimfindevermögen von säugetieren. II. Versuche on Mäusen. *Z. Tierpsychol.* **12**, 452–8.

LORD, F. E. (1941) A study of spatial orientation of children. *J. educ. Res.* **34**, 481–505.

LUCANNAS, F. VON (1924) On the sense of locality in men and animals. *Rev. Revs.* **70**, 218.

LUND, F. H. (1930) Physical asymmetries and disorientation. *Am. J. Psychol.* **42**, 51–62.

MAGAREY, A. T. (1899) Tracking by the Australian aborigine. *Proc. Roy. Geogr. Soc. Australasia,* **3**, 120.

MATHER, J. G. and BAKER, R. R. (1980) A demonstration of navigation by rodents using an orientation cage. *Nature, Lond.* **284**, 259–62.

MATTHEWS, G. V. T. (1955) *Bird navigation* (1st. ed.) University Press, Cambridge.

MATTHEWS, G. V. T. (1968) *Bird navigation* (2nd. ed.) University Press, Cambridge.

MENZEL, E. W., PREMACK, D. and WOODRUFF, G. (1978) Map reading by chimpanzees. *Folia Primat.* **29**, 241–9.

MOORE, F. (1977) Geomagnetic disturbance and the orientation of nocturnally migrating birds. *Science*, **196**, 682–4.

MOORE, F. (1978) Sunset and the orientation of a nocturnal migrant bird. *Nature, Lond.* **274**, 154–6.

O'KEEFE, J. and NADEL, L. (1979) *The hippocampus as a cognitive map.* Oxford University Press, London.

OLTON, D. S. (1977) Spatial memory. *Sci. Amer.* **236**, 82–98.

PAPI, F. (1976) The olfactory navigation system of homing pigeons. *Verh. Deut. Zool. Ges.* **1976**, 184–205.

PAPI, F., IOALÉ, P., FIASCHI, V., BENVENUTI, S. and BALDACCINI, N. E. (1974) Olfactory navigation of pigeons: the effect of treatment with odorous air currents. *J. Comp. Physiol.* **94**, 187–93.

PAPI, F., IOALÉ, P., FIASCHI, V., BENVENUTI, S. and BALDACCINI, N. E. (1978) Pigeon homing: cue detection during outward journey and initial orientation. *In*: Schmidt-Koenig, K. and Keeton, W. T. (eds) *Animal migration, navigation and homing.* Springer, Heidelberg. pp. 65–77.

REBACH, S. (1978) The role of celestial cues in short range migrations of the hermit crab, *Pagurus longicarpus. Anim. Behav.* **26**, 835–42.

RICHARDSON, W. J. (1978) Timing and amount of bird migration in relation to weather: a review. *Oikos* **30**, 224–72.

SAILA, S. B. and SHAPPY, R. A. (1963) Random movement and orientation in salmon migration. *J. Cons. perm. int. Explor. Mar.* **128**, 153–66.

SARGENT, T. D. (1962) A study of homing in the bank swallow (*Riparia riparia*). *Auk* **79**, 234–46.

SCHMIDT-KOENIG, K. (1979) *Avian orientation and navigation.* Academic Press, London.

SCHMIDT-KOENIG, K. and KEETON, W. T. (1977) Sun compass utilization by pigeons wearing frosted contact lenses. *Auk.* **94**, 143–5.

SCHMIDT-KOENIG, K. and KEETON, W. T. (eds) (1978) *Animal migration, navigation and homing.* Springer, Heidelberg.

SOTTHIBANDHU, S. and BAKER, R. R. (1979) Celestial orientation by the large yellow underwing moth, *Noctua pronuba.* L. *Anim. Behav.* **27**, 786–800.

SOUTHERN, W. E. (1971) Comments at a meeting. *Ann. N.Y. Acad. Sci.* **188**, 337.

SUPA, M., COTZIN, M. and DALLENBACH, K. M. (1944) 'Facial vision': the perception of obstacles by the blind. *Am. J. Psychol.* **57**, 133–83.

VIGUIER, C. (1882) Le sens de l'orientation et ses organs chez les animaux et chez l'homme. *Rev. philomath.* **14**, 1–36.

WAGNER, G. (1972) Topography and pigeon orientation. *In*: Galler, S. R., Schmidt-Koenig, K., Jacobs, G. J. and Belleville, R. E. (eds) *Animal orientation and navigation.* NASA SP-262 US Govt. Printing Office, Washington D.C. pp. 249–73.

WALCOTT, C. (1978) Anomalies in the earth's magnetic field increase the scatter of pigeon's vanishing bearings. *In*: Schmidt-Koenig, K. and Keeton, W. T. (eds) *Animal migration, navigation and homing* Springer, Heidelberg. pp. 143–51.

WALCOTT, C., GOULD, J. L., KIRSCHVINK, J. L. (1979) Pigeons have magnets. *Science* **205**, 1027–8.

WALCOTT, C. and GREEN, R. P. (1974) Orientation of homing pigeons altered by a change in the direction of an applied magnetic field. *Science* **184**, 180–2.

WALLRAFF, H. G. (1978) Preferred compass directions in initial orientation of homing pigeons. *In*: Schmidt-Koenig, K. and Keeton, W. T. (eds) *Animal migration, navigation and homing*. Springer, Heidelberg. pp. 171–83.

WARREN, H. C. (1908) Magnetic sense of direction. *Psychol. Bull.* **5**, 376–7.

WHITEN, A. (1978) Operant studies of pigeon orientation and navigation. *Anim. Behav.* **26**, 571–610.

WILKINSON, D. H. (1952) The random element in bird 'navigation'. *J. exp. Biol.* **29**, 532–60.

WILLCOX, W. F. (1940) *Studies in American demography*. Cornell University Press, Ithaca.

WILLIAMS, T. C. and WILLIAMS, J. M. (1970) Radio tracking of homing and feeding flights of a neotropical bat, *Phyllostomus hastatus. Anim. Behav.* **18**, 302–9.

WILLIAMSON, T. (1979) Dowsing achieves new credence. *New Scientist.* **81**, 371–3.

WILSON, E. O. (1975) *Sociobiology, the new synthesis*. Belknap Press, Harvard.

WILTSCHKO, R. and WILTSCHKO, W. (1978) Evidence for the use of magnetic outward-journey information in homing pigeons. *Naturwiss.* **65**, 112–13.

WILTSCHKO, R., WILTSCHKO, W. and KEETON, W. T., (1978) Effect of outward journey in an altered magnetic field in young homing pigeons. *In*: Schmidt-Koenig, K. and Keeton, W. T. (eds) *Animal migration, navigation and homing*. Springer, Heidelberg. pp. 152–61.

WILTSCHKO, W. and WILTSCHKO, R. (1976) Interrelation of magnetic compass and star orientation in night-migrating birds. *J. Comp. Physiol.* **109**, 91–9.

WILTSCHKO, W. and WILTSCHKO, R. (1978) A theoretical model for migratory orientation and homing in birds. *Oikos* **30**, 177–87.

WORCHEL, P. (1951) Space perception and orientation in the blind. *Psychol. Monogr.* **65**(332).

WORCHEL, P. (1952) The role of vestibular organs in space orientation. *J. exp. Psychol.* **44**, 4–10.

WRANGEL, F. von (1840) *Narrative of an expedition to the Polar Sea in 1820–23*. Robinson, London.

WYON, J. B. and GORDON, J. E. (1971) *The Khanna Study: population problems in the rural Punjab*. Harvard, Cambridge.

ZACHARIAH, K. C. (1968) *Migrants in Greater Bombay*. Asia Publishing House, London.

Index